SOCIETY
AND THE
HEALTHY HOMOSEXUAL

Dr. George Weinberg is a practicing psychotherapist, and has long been involved in the movement to educate the public on the issue of homosexuality. His writings have appeared in numerous technical journals and popular magazines, and he is the author of *The Action Approach,* a popular study on personality.

Society
and the
Healthy Homosexual

by DR. GEORGE WEINBERG

Anchor Books
Anchor Press/Doubleday
Garden City, New York

Society and the Healthy Homosexual was originally published in hardcover by St. Martin's Press, Inc. This edition is published by arrangement with St. Martin's Press.

Anchor Books edition: 1973

" 'O day and night, but this is wondrous strange.'
'And therefore as a stranger give it welcome.' "

—*Hamlet*

CONTENTS

ACKNOWLEDGMENTS

A great many people contributed to the completion of this book. I wish to thank Dr. Catharine Stimpson, Alice Fennessey, Leslie Pockell, Dr. C. A. Tripp and Edith Efron, who gave me important editorial suggestions along the way. Also Lige Clarke and Jack Nichols, editors of *Gay,* who have always given me a free hand in writing for their newspaper. Some of the pieces in this book have been adapted from articles which first appeared there.

The people who spent long hours discussing various concepts with me are too numerous for a complete list of them to be given here. Among them are old friends: Kay Tobin, author of *The Gay Crusaders;* Dr. Franklin Kameny; Lilli Vincenz and a group of about fifteen lesbians active for civil rights in Washington, D.C. Also Arthur Evans of the Gay Activists Alliance in New York City, which has moved with stunning rapidity in its effort to erase discrimination against homosexuals; and various of the staff members of several publications also dedicated to this purpose. As for my knowledge of "unhealthy homosexuals," this comes primarily from my psychotherapy practice, rather than from my personal acquaintanceships with homosexual men and women, who properly do not believe they are in need of psychotherapy.

The prevailing attitude toward homosexuals in the U.S. and many other countries is revulsion and hostility. Forty-five of our fifty states still punish homosexuals by long imprisonment for acts entered into in private by consenting adults. Only a tiny fraction of homosexuals have ever actually been arrested, but the public attitude, reflected in the legal codes of the different states, has even wider implications. At present, it is not unconstitutional to deny housing to a person who is a known homosexual, or to refuse a job to such a person for this reason. Indeed, many large corporations have the avowed policy of refusing to employ homosexuals, and so does the Federal Government. All this, mind you, for acts and desires not harmful to anyone.

Such discriminatory practices against homosexuals have deep psychological motives, which I shall be discussing in this book.

In recent years, certain mental health experts espousing the popular attitude toward homosexuals have written that homosexuals are mentally ill, and this idea has caught on. Some of these experts have shown an unexpected eagerness to denounce anyone who says that homosexuals can and often do live happily. Evidence that many of these experts are themselves motivated by the conventional attitude of revulsion is to be found in their very opposition to the notion that such persons exist. If they truly considered homosexuality an illness and nothing more, they would have no complaint with the dissemination of the point of view that one can live with it and be happy. It would be uplifting to hear someone say, "Homosexuality is what you make of it."

One need only contact any of the gay liberation groups, like the Gay Activists Alliance, the Gay Liberation Front, the Mattachine Society, The Daughters of Bilitis, in the big cities, or the hundreds of other groups assembled on college campuses around the country, to get in touch with homosexual men and women who are enjoying their lives. Not all who work in these movements are healthy by everyone's definition, but among the members of these groups there are many persons who are homosexual and not suffering from fear, guilt or regret, and who in other critical respects qualify as healthy. These are people capable of expressing love and enjoying the love of others; many of them are people who feel deep commitment to humanity and the willingness to work for its betterment.

Of course, only a tiny minority of the estimated fifteen million homosexuals in this country are actively participating in the movement for homosexuals' rights. The great majority prefer, like the rest of mankind, to lead their own lives and pursue their own goals privately. I mention these groups only because they make some of their personnel available for discussion with persons interested to see whether homosexuals like those I mentioned really exist. The experts who consider homosexuality a sickness virtually never get in touch with these groups for people to interview, and content themselves with basing their assertions on the testimony of troubled homosexuals who seek psychiatric help.

It is not surprising that homosexuals themselves often suffer from the conventional attitude of revulsion and anger toward things homosexual. In their case the problem is even more serious than elsewhere—the attitude is a condemnation of self. In the case of these people, the problem is not oppression but their own harsh evaluation of themselves for being homosexual. The essential issue is not whether one is homosexual but how the person handles his homosexuality if he is. As Kinsey often said, a major problem for therapists should be to determine why some people regarded as deviates remain tormented while others are able to go on and live successful lives.

This book is in part an examination of a disease called homophobia—an attitude held by many non-homosexuals and perhaps by the majority of homosexuals in countries where there is discrimination against homosexuals.

As a psychotherapist, I have had as an aim to help nonhomosexuals rid themselves of this attitude for their own sakes, for reasons I shall be discussing. Also, while working extensively with homosexual men and women, my purpose has been to help them overcome this attitude, where it has existed. It has been to enable them to become healthy homosexuals. This has entailed helping homosexuals in our phobic society to accept themselves and to regard their own homosexual desires as valid. The premise is that in a truly great society there is room for all who do not infringe on the rights of others.

ONE

HOMOPHOBIA

I would never consider a patient healthy unless he had overcome his prejudice against homosexuality. Of course if the person is himself homosexual, the prejudice he holds is barring the way to easy expression of his own desires. But even if he is heterosexual, his repugnance at homosexuality is certain to be harmful to him. In my experience, such a prejudice is more rife among heterosexual men than among heterosexual women.

The person who belittles homosexuals with evident enjoyment is at the very least telling me that he wants to establish his own sense of importance through contrast with other people—a tenuous business. He says with revulsion that someone he knows is "a faggot," or he lowers his voice when describing a sexual advance that a man once made to him.

Do you know how certain female impersonation clubs survive? Nonhomosexual men, who want to convince themselves and their wives or girl friends of their masculinity, throng them.

They sit at ringside—or pay one of the transvestites to come over and sit with them. They pinch the lesbians and ask jocularly, "Are you a boy or a girl?" Some of them chew fat cigars. When the stage show begins and the drag queens come out, they whistle. The lion is allowing the lamb to live and bleat.

At three o'clock in the morning our so-called head of the household says raucously, "Check please!" and overtips the waitress. On the stairway he puts his arm around his woman's waist. He is assuring her by his firm hold that he is with her, that the time has come when he is to take her away from this sordid atmosphere.

On the street he mutters something to the effect that the people below are sick and "really sad." He finds a cab immediately, since the customers in such places are known to be showoffs with money, and a line of cabs is waiting for people like him. In the cab he smooches with his woman and they feel like a normal couple.

This is the identity that the patient who slurs homosexuality assumes in my mind while he is talking. He is bracing himself and trying to bolster his relationship by presenting it against a contrast. But in so doing, he is increasing his fear of sordidness—and heightening his fear of witnessing human variety.

Moreover, he is inhibiting himself. He is depriving himself not of homosexual experiences, which he truthfully does not want, but of all else that he connects with homosexuality. For instance, he makes it impossible to have friends who are homosexual, and thus loses the possible benefit of a viewpoint that would have widened his. And if he regards even so natural an attitude as passivity as homosexual, he has sentenced himself to renouncing receptivity as an attitude for himself.

This last is a very severe loss. A fellow looked at a reproduction of Michelangelo's painting of Adam on the wall of my office, and turning away, told me he hated it.

"Why?" I asked.

"He's too passive. He's not doing anything."

"Well, he was just created, seconds ago. He's got a good excuse," I said.

"That doesn't matter," he said bluntly, and he turned away in disgust from perhaps the finest nude ever drawn, sickened because the character was delicate and lolling, doing nothing more than absorbing experience.

Most men who loathe homosexuals have a deathly fear of abandonment in the direction of passivity. The surrender of control signifies to them a loss of masculinity, and their demand for control produces narrowness. To condemn passivity is like condemning your eyeballs. We need passivity to see, to discover, to learn.

The person I am describing usually feels under tremendous pressure to be the aggressor in sex, and he expects conformity and passivity on the part of his woman. He is easily undone when he does not find it. He inflicts ludicrous role-expectations on his children. In some cases the fear of being in any way womanish has so invaded the crannies of the person's mind that it affects his attitudes toward the use of color in his

home and in his clothing. He has almost defined himself out of existence by the very contrast he is fighting
so hard to establish.

If a son is homosexual, he goes berserk. To reassure
himself that he himself has not also succumbed, and is
still tough, he might take a punch at the boy. "That
fellow is never coming into this house again!" he shouts
at his wife, his eyes popping, after the boy has stormed
out. It seems unmanning to him to have given birth
to an unmanly son.

I am describing a clear-cut but prevalent form of
phobia. It has not been identified as such by the experts because the sufferer's viewpoint jibes with most
experts' opinions that homosexuals are disturbed. If
we liken homosexuality to an illness, the father's distress looks reasonable. We expect despair and hair-
pulling when someone close to us is desperately ill.
But why his assault? One does not assault someone
merely because he is ill. One assaults him because one
is mortally afraid of him.

What causes homophobia—the dread of being in
close quarters with homosexuals—and in the case of
homosexuals themselves, self-loathing? Volumes have
been written—by psychologists, sexologists, anthro-
pologists, sociologists, and physiologists—on homosexuality, its origins and its development. This is because in most western civilizations, homosexuality is
itself considered a problem; our unwarranted distress
over homosexuality is not classified as a problem because it is still a majority point of view. Homophobia
is still part of the conventional American attitude.

Despite massive evidence that homosexuals are as
various in their personalities as anyone else, the public

at this time still holds many misconceptions which in some cases are thought to justify our discriminatory practices. Among these misconceptions are the belief that homosexuals seduce young children (child molestation is preponderantly a heterosexual practice); the belief that homosexuals are untrustworthy; that homosexual men hate women; that homosexual women hate men—all beliefs unsupported by evidence, but held unquestioningly by millions.

If there is any doubt of the existence of homophobia, consider that in England and the U.S., for hundreds of years, homosexuality was unmentionable. In the courts, homosexual crimes were alluded to in Latin, or implied by circuitous language, and judges have sentenced people to languish in jail for acts considered so vile that they should not be talked about. For this reason, homosexuality has sometimes been called "the crime without a name."

There is a certain cost in suffering from any phobia, and that is that the inhibition spreads to a whole circle of acts related to the feared activity, in reality or symbolically. In this case, acts imagined to be conducive to homosexual feelings, or that are reminiscent of homosexual acts, are shunned. Since homosexuality is more feared by men than women, this results in marked differences in permissiveness toward the sexes. For instance, a great many men refrain from embracing each other or kissing each other, and women do not. Moreover, men do not as a rule express fondness for each other, or longing for each other's company, as openly as women do. Men tend not to permit themselves to see beauty in the physical forms of other men, or enjoy it; whereas women may openly express admiration for the beauty of other women. Men, even lifetime friends, will not sit as close together on a couch while talking earnestly as women may; they will not look into each other's faces as steadily or as fondly. Ramifications of this phobic fear extend even to parent-child relationships. Millions of fathers feel that it would not befit them to kiss their sons affectionately or embrace them, whereas mothers can kiss and embrace their daughters as well as their sons.

The fear of homosexuality is inculcated in early life. Studies have been done in which children are asked to place paper figures on a background, to indicate the degree of closeness between imaginary persons represented by the figures. The children are asked to indicate that the play figures like each other, or are acquaintances, or are frightened of each other. In one study, sixth-grade boys and girls were subjects, and the cutouts were of children their own age. The girls showed a strong tendency to indicate fondness by putting the cutouts close to each other; by comparison, the boys did not put the cutouts of boys near to each other. The differences were so systematic as to meet stringent scientific criteria. The researcher concluded:

> It is common knowledge that in our society females are allowed to assume closer physical interaction distances than males are. . . . Sex differences in interpersonal spacing have been found on numerous occasions . . . and observation shows that females can tolerate closer physical presences than males in this culture. (Guardo)*

Society's fear of intimacy between males has implications far beyond the sexual realm. Apparently, boys

* References for authorities cited appear on pp. 141–144.

learn it by the age of eleven, and it results in a significant deprivation of freedom for them. For instance, millions of heterosexual men who suffer from homophobia find it almost impossible to gaze at the bodies of other men, though they are understandably curious about them.

An Australian psychiatrist named Dr. N. McConaghy conducted a study typical of many in which the aim was to help perfect a device for spotting homosexuals. In this study, he puts the penis of each of his subjects into an apparatus designed to measure whether it expanded or contracted as the subjects viewed pictures of nude men and women engaging in somewhat suggestive acts, like towelling themselves. Eleven heterosexual medical students served as the controls for a homosexual population. In responding to the pictures of the nude males, the penises of the heterosexual young medical students shrank! One understands easily why they did not expand, since presumably the medical students were not erotically aroused at the sight of the nude males. But why did they shrink? The answer is: fear. And consider the implication of this. If the sight of the naked body of the male had this effect on the medical students, how will it influence them as practitioners, when they will be called upon to look at and handle the naked bodies of men?

When a phobia incapacitates a person from engaging in activities considered decent by a society, the person himself is the sufferer. He loses out on the chance to go skiing perhaps, if it is acrophobia, or the chance to take the elevator to the street each day if it is claustrophobia. But here the phobia appears as antagonism directed toward a particular group of people. Inevitably, it leads to disdain of those people, and to mistreatment of them. This phobia in operation is a prejudice, which means that we can widen our understanding of it by considering the phobia from the point of view of its being a prejudice and uncovering its chief motives.

Here are the chief ones that I have been able to identify. There are five of them.

The Religious Motive

In his celebrated work *The Nature of Prejudice,* Gordon Allport tells of having examined numerous definitions of prejudice. Each definition refers to an "unfounded judgment" with an accompanying "feeling tone." Technically, a prejudice may be pro or con, but as Allport intimates, the word "prejudice" is applied almost exclusively to antagonistic attitudes. Allport thoughtfully defines a prejudice as "an avertive or hostile attitude toward a person who belongs to a group, simply because he belongs to that group, and is therefore presumed to have the objectionable qualities ascribed to the group."

In accounting for attitudes of long standing in a society, the approach of historians is to identify the forces that introduced the attitude back in the past.

Much of our present tradition around homosexuality, and sexuality generally, goes back to the Judaeo-Christian code. The Biblical stricture against "spilling the seed" covered homosexuality too, and there are explicit prohibitions against homosexuality in the Bible. Oppression of homosexuals became most atrocious when ecclesiastic powers brought their backing to it. As part of its wider campaign against pleasure, the Church evolved an enormously strict system. The Christian ideal was complete celibacy—accompanied by a craving for asceticism, purity and poverty. For hundreds of years Christianity set itself to distinguishing possible sources of pleasure and prohibiting them.

Not even sexual intercourse between husband and wife for procreation was fully above reproach. The Church catalogued variants of that act too, and banned most of them in the belief that they involved choices aimed at enjoyment. It banned nudity, and the sexual intercourse position using entry from the rear, because this position was thought unduly pleasurable. To implement its bans, Christianity set up its own courts and developed its own brand of law, called *canon law*. Whereas *common law* was concerned chiefly with protecting people from damage inflicted by others, canon law dealt with offenses to the Church. It punished people for actions that harmed no one, and justified itself by calling them sinful and arguing that they were damaging to the performer. Supposedly for their own sakes, thousands found guilty of homosexual acts were executed. As an obvious seeker for sexual pleasure without the excuse of child-getting, the homosexual came to seem a living rebuke to Christianity. Under its influence, emperors borrowed the tactic of putting homosexuals to death, and the public embraced this view of homosexuals as heretics and sinners.

The great attraction of the Church was its professed power to remit sins. Its followers' very observance of Christianity in all its detail renewed in them their belief in eternal damnation as a possibility for them after death. By renouncing pleasure and condemning those who sought it, they kept alive the belief that enjoyment itself is detrimental to one's chances for escaping Hell.

The influence of ecclesiastical thinking is still to be found, not just among Christians but everywhere among us. Sometimes the Bible itself is blamed for this. But, as the Reverend Troy Perry notes in public appearances, those who base their condemnation of homosexuality on Biblical admonitions are exercising considerable personal judgment over which Biblical teachings to accept and which to disregard. Perry often refers to Leviticus, where the recommendation is made that two men who engage in a homosexual act should be stoned. He observes that in the same book of the Bible, it is said to be wrong for a woman to wear a scarlet dress or for anyone to eat shrimp. And yet people who wear scarlet and eat shrimp continue to cite Leviticus as their authority for condemning homosexuality.

Reverend Perry, who is pastor of the Metropolitan Community Church in Los Angeles, is the best known of an increasing number of religious leaders who give services for homosexuals. In only two years Perry won a following of 16,000 homosexuals in eleven major cities in the United States. The main issue for these men and women is not whether one believes in God, but whether belief in God is incompatible with homosexuality. Reverend Perry's own answer is repeated as a chant by those who attend his services: "The Lord is my Shepherd and He knows I'm gay." To blame the Church alone for the phobic attitude toward sexuality held today is to overlook ongoing dynamic attitudes, which must always be present in a population when a prejudice persists.

The Secret Fear of Being Homosexual

A second motive for the homophobic reaction is the fear of being homosexual oneself.

When Dick Leitsch, who was then head of the New York Mattachine Society for the rights of homosexuals, was on a speaking tour of the colleges, he would sometimes encounter opposition in an unexpected form. At Ohio University in Athens, a man stood up out of the audience and roared at him after his speech: "But you see, Mr. Leitsch, if you take the laws away, and the social stigmas too, against homosexuals, then everyone will be homosexual." Apparently, the man perceived the law as a vital help in deterring him from becoming homosexual himself.

Similarly, in discussing a file clerk who, for homosexual acts committed as a minor, had been fired from his job as an adult and was later reinstated, Presidential Assistant Walter W. Jenkins, gave assurance in 1964 that the man "would not actually control air traffic." Months later, this very man who had tacitly granted the irresponsibility of homosexuals left the government after being discovered in a homosexual act.

In both cases we see what Freud called *reaction formation,* the mechanism of defending against an impulse in oneself by taking a stand against its expression by others.

There are many cases of prejudice as part of reaction formation. In fact, some leaders of the homophile movement believe that the most vociferous enemies of homosexuals are combatting homosexual urges in themselves. However, my own study suggests that the motives are usually more complicated than the mere concern with being homosexual.

Repressed Envy

The third motive for homophobia is repressed envy.

"An outstanding result of studies of bigoted personalities seems to be the discovery of a sharp cleavage between conscious and unconscious layers" (Allport). The prejudiced person harbors ideas about himself that he does not express. The dangerous constellation is of the form, *I am successful because I am thought to possess some particular attribute, but I fear I am deficient in it.*

Two kinds of vulnerability are possible here. The person may see someone who shakes his confidence regarding how much of the attribute he possesses. A would-be competitor looms in front of him. Threat of this form has been discussed occasionally in connection with the prejudice against blacks. The argument is made that some white men rest their sense of security on the belief that they are supreme as lovers; believing that blacks have special sexual prowess, they downgrade black men in order to deny them the right to competition.

But the imagined vulnerability is of a different form where homosexuals are feared. *The homosexual is felt to belie the importance of the attributes themselves.* The homosexual man does not seem to be saying, "I can do better with women than you." He seems to be saying, "Your success with women isn't nearly so important for happiness as you imagine. And look at all you've sacrificed for it." Of "masculinity" he seems to be saying, "That attribute of yours means nothing! Here I am with no desire to possess it."

The homosexual man is much more apt to be regarded as threatening on this score than the homosexual woman. Most men are taught from early childhood that to engage in homosexual acts would be to surrender their "masculine identity." Women are not, by analogy, imagined to be less feminine if they engage in homosexual love-making, and moreover, they do not learn to fear the loss of their identity as much. After years of struggle to achieve a precarious masculine identity, many heterosexual men feel threatened by the sight of homosexuals, who appear to them to be disdainful of the basic requirements of manhood.

To these men, personal success appears to demand that they go on conveying an impression of themselves which is so far from the fact that they cannot possibly manage it perfectly. There appear to be numerous requirements. For instance, they envision the successful man as perennially confident, as dressing well and appropriately at all times, as making a good living, as commanding respect from his wife, and as in command of "where he is going." Without respite, this would-be ideal American man must toil to appear as what he knows he is not; and since he is apt to believe that lapses *should disqualify* him from enjoying the culture's rewards and even from love, he is particularly disturbed by the sight of someone who apparently feels no need to assert himself in the same ways. Puritanism was once defined by H. L. Mencken as "the lurking fear that someone somewhere is happy"; and surprising as it sounds, this fear often operates in the heterosexual's view of the homosexual.

Despite their social role as outcasts, homosexual men, and often homosexual women too, are thought by a surprising number of people to have it *easier* than others and become the objects of suppressed envy. In cases where being a responsible head of a household is thought of as a requisite for sex or family pleasures, where courtship is thought of as the minimum payment for sex, and where sex itself is sanctioned only as a means of propagating the race, it vexes people to see others apparently matching the profits without having to pay as dearly for them. The laws branding homosexuality a crime are felt to restore the balance somewhat, but not enough for some people.

Homosexual women appear to suffer less from this sort of envy than homosexual men do. Perhaps this is because "many men regard the lesbian choice as that of a lesser for a lesser," as feminist leader Dr. Catharine Stimpson put it.

Besides, the machinery of discrimination against lesbians has been able to grind quietly. By granting numerous social privileges and responsibilities to women only if they married, societies have uniformly punished lesbians without even having to acknowledge that they existed. In addition, many men, and perhaps those who tend to dislike lesbians most, pride themselves on being charitable toward women. For ages, homage to women has been serving men as a sign of their own decency, and has often been used to justify ruthlessness elsewhere. One doesn't punch lesbians with impunity for the same reason one doesn't kill women and children, according to the rules of war. Probably for this reason more than others, lesbians have been spared the more pointed and brutal kinds of attacks that have been made on homosexual men. On the whole, repressed envy operates more as a motive for the abuse of homosexual men than of homosexual women.

The Threat to Values

Another motive for resentment toward homosexuals is that they are seen as constituting a threat to one's values.

Anyone who does not adopt a society's usual value system runs the risk of being seen as undermining the society. Because the person does not share the interests and goals of the majority, there is suspicion of him. This remains so, even if the person produces as much as others and works as hard over a lifetime. The mere fact of the homosexual's not striving for marriage, for example, makes it harder to include him or her in appeals made to the populace. Failure to be swayed by the usual value system is apt to present a problem to large-scale movers—like the Federal Government, for instance—or to any industry that appeals to people in large numbers. The Federal tax systems would need marked revision to apply equitably to homosexuals. It is always easiest for big organizations like insurance companies to make their pitch to large numbers of people when they can appeal to common values. In a sixty-second commercial, we see a fire destroying a house and a family being reimbursed. Such an ostensibly universal commercial does not apply to homosexuals, and indeed it is interesting to note how many TV commercials are inapplicable to homosexual men and women, even when they are purchasers of the products advertised.

The rift between homosexuals and others in this respect bears close analogy to certain aspects of the so-called generation gap. Underlying it is a severe clash of values, with resultant rage toward those considered nonconformists. For ages, our national banners have had the same ideas emblazoned on them—"Marriage," "A Good Job," "A Good Family Name," "Money." For not marching in file behind these banners millions have been called alienated, rebellious. This is a charge homosexuals have often had made against them.

Existence Without Vicarious Immortality

Finally, by getting patients to free-associate at length, I have discovered a strange and poignant reason for the phobia.

The notion that there are homosexuals distresses some people because the thought of persons without children reawakens their fear of death. Today in the larger population, vicarious immortality through having children and grandchildren assuages the spirit of millions and blunts the edge of mortality for them. Our great glorification of reproduction, with all the customs and modes that advance it, serves in part as a ceremony to circumvent death as if by magic. The decision by a person not to have children opens up the concern in many minds, "What about death? How can he live with the knowledge that he is going to leave no one behind?" It jars these people to think that the homosexual may not be concerned with leaving "his own flesh and blood" after him. Whether or not the homosexual man or woman has had children in a particular case, the person's very existence becomes a fearful reminder to people of what life would be like without children.

In many minds, how to react to homosexuals becomes a contest of whether to show loyalty to the individual or to the family as the smallest possible unit. "Homosexuals are the only major oppressed minority that cannot present itself in the endearing constellation of a family group." This is how writer Alice Fennessey put it. The tender sight of parents and little ones has won mercy for many groups; in fact, the most fearsome animals in the zoo, those reputed to be the deadliest, steal gentle feelings from us when we see them in family groups—the bear licking her cubs, the tiger nursing her kittens and snarling when we come too close.

The homosexual cannot lay claim to this sort of sympathy. Indeed, the adversaries of homosexuals have done what they could to make homosexuals appear as outright enemies of the family. The coincidental loss of one's role as a mother or father, a loss common but far from universal among homosexuals, is made to seem the consequence of a willful, ugly choice, one motivated by hatred of the family.

Observe how preoccupation with the nuclear family, and the blind faith in reproduction as the standard for sexuality, and the religious motive, tie together. Reproduction and children and the promise of an afterlife are utilized by some as magical devices to cope with the fear of death. To many, the homosexual, who does not appear to be wearing these amulets, evokes this fear.

Those who shun homosexuals tend to share a number of unstated assumptions, of which the most important is that something is frighteningly wrong when a human being diverges from the standardized pattern of existence. Some, especially the uneducated, are still apt to express their attitude with open, ugly hostility: by jibes and insults, or by actually beating up homosexuals. More insidious in its way is the disguised hostility of many who consider themselves enlightened and educated, this hostility is often concealed by the device of shifting the irrational fear to an intellectual level and presenting it as if it were rational. Perhaps the most usual expression of this is an endless absorption with the question: How did the homosexual get that way? This ostensibly valid intellectual inquiry is frequently an expression of hostilities or fears, which become presented as if they were part of a serious intellectual exploration.

The fact is that the combination of physiological readiness and social experience resulting in the development of *any* erotic preference—homosexual or heterosexual—is so intricate that science has not been able to fathom it as yet. No group of experts in any field can predict who will be homosexual, though after the fact, psychologists of nearly every school stand ready to pontificate to individuals about how they became homosexual. The homosexual man or woman who goes to psychologists using six different approaches will hear six different explanations of how he or she became homosexual.

It is noteworthy that we seldom hear the question: How did a person become heterosexual? Probably we shall discover the answers to the two questions at the same time, if we ever do, since the real issue is: How does one learn sexual preference? The origin of homosexuality comes into question because it is considered a deviant course. What pebble diverted the stream? As if without proof it were assumed that the capacity to reproduce sets the standard in sexual conduct from which one should not deviate—that, therefore, heterosexuality must in some profound sense be in the mainstream of thought and activity in the life of every individual and homosexuality a sign of interference. The truth is that reproduction is seldom the motive for sexual activity and that the human range of sexual possibilities develops independently of the desire to reproduce.

Consistent with the tendency for brutality against homosexuals to be directed toward men more than toward women is the fact that inquiries about origin are more apt to be concerned with male homosexuality than female homosexuality. Probably because society accords many special benefits to men, it is considered worse for a man to "act like a woman" than the reverse. For instance, it is considered worse for a man to dress like a woman than vice versa.

> The differential cultural tolerance for cross-sex behavior displayed by males and females illustrates the role of sex characteristics in the assignment of symptomatic status to deviant behavior patterns. The wearing of female apparel by males is considered to be indicative of a serious psychological disorder, requiring prompt legal and psychiatric attention. On the other hand, females may adopt masculine garb, hair styles, and a wide range of characteristically masculine response patterns without being labeled as mentally disturbed. Since masculine role behavior occupies a position of relatively high prestige and power in our society, and often is more generously rewarded than feminine role behavior, the

emulation of masculine tendencies by females is more understandable and, therefore, less likely to be interpreted by reference to disease processes. (Bandura)

If it is a man, he has surrendered a great advantage. His expected role-behavior entitles him to prestige and power. "He would have to be crazy to give all that away. He must be crazy." This is the reasoning. In contrast, the woman has merely caught on to the way the game is being played. She is trying to pass as a man for the obvious reward—just as some fellow on the *Titanic* tried to pass as a woman when they were the only ones being given access to life rafts. From the assumption that everyone craves the same social advantages, one could conclude nothing else. The as yet unfathomable complexity of an identity choice, or of sexual arousal generally, ceases to be a problem. All is explained by viewing the lesbian and the heterosexual woman who likes "masculine attire" as being insincere in their preference and merely using it as a canny device to gain social advantage.

Implicit in all this is the unwarranted assumption that at bottom we all crave the same ends and advantages. In the last analysis, the homophobic reaction I have been describing is a form of acute conventionality. Ultimately, it condemns because of difference. It has every basic attribute of an irrational social prejudice.

TWO

THE BIAS OF PSYCHOANALYSIS

The homosexual is not told like the black that he is stupid. He is not told like the Jew that he is mercenary. The almost invariable expression of disdain for homosexuals is that they are neurotic, "sick"—that the homosexual has a malformed psyche. Many homosexuals have accepted this as true, and suffer because of a bias held against themselves. Since the case against homosexuals varies every few years as psychological and medical orientations change, it would be hopeless to try to refute such charges. Besides, the burden should not be on homosexuals to acquit themselves of these charges, but on those who make them to produce evidence in support of them. Where a person is not harming himself and not harming other people, the assertion that he is psychologically sick is meaningless.

Yet millions of homosexual men and women have

embraced the view of themselves as sick, and in the nineteen-fifties even representatives of the homophile movement in public appearances would sometimes stand up and stutter and plead that they could not answer with certainty the question whether they were sick. No one can answer such a question with certainty, heterosexual or homosexual. Nor should an accused person automatically become a defendant, for if he does the burden will fall on him to define sickness and acquit himself of all charges. Actually the time has come for accusers to do some fast talking if they intend to go on professing theories that disparage individuals and provide the rationale for prejudices.

By far the most sweeping influence on the prevalent view of the homosexual as a mental health phenomenon is psychoanalysis. To multitudes psychoanalysis has appeared to stand independently as a body of knowledge. But in fact its conclusions, and especially those about homosexuals, are merely restatements of the Judaeo-Christian code already discussed. Only the ostensible methods of arriving at these conclusions are different.

Freud was more influenced by prevailing Judaeo-Christian attitudes than he thought. For instance, his demand that the sex act be aimed at procreation led to an overstress on coitus, and the restriction that the act be between man and wife. The further from possibly being reproductive a sex act was, the further from being permissible. To see how closely Freud's outlook resembled the prevailing view, one need only consider that what was illegal, in Freud's day and now, became "neurotic" or "perverted" in psychoanalytic terms.

Sodomy, oral-genital contacts, homosexuality, all widely punishable by law, are classified by psychoanalysis as perversions.

Even the overstress on sex in psychoanalysis has its precedent. Of the thirty-six crimes in Mosaic law punishable by death, one half involve sexual relations of one kind or another.

Psychoanalysis holds that sexuality has inherent aims, and not merely learned ones. It assumes that the one natural course awaiting all of us is heterosexuality and fulfillment through becoming a parent. It says that ultimately the best sex act is coitus, and failure to accept this signifies that a person has not matured properly through the different stages of development. A healthy person is supposedly one who makes the choice of heterosexuality and whose preferred act is coitus. Oral-genital acts between man and woman need not indicate faulty development if kept to their place as part of foreplay leading to coitus. Homosexual acts can have no such defense. They are obviously not designed for procreation. Therefore, consistent with his bias, Freud considered homosexuality an illness, though one nearly impossible to cure. Everywhere, the prevailing ethic regarding sexual acts manifested itself almost identically in the law and in psychoanalysis, the difference being that acts criminal in one case were considered signs of faulty character development in the other.

For Freud, there were four main ways one becomes homosexual. The first is *fixation*. The person fails to develop along a course, on which he would proceed naturally. Fixation is overinvestment in some particular phase of development, with consequent failure to move

past it. Freud's image for this was an army marching.
The general who leaves too many men at an early stopping place will find his army too weak to proceed. The
assumption is that there are fixed stages of development, which can be charted for a person before he is
born. One will predictably hold a sequence of predilec-
tions for pleasure in different forms. However, it is
expected that the healthy person will not fixate at any
of these earlier pleasures but will continue on to full
heterosexuality.

Today it is believed by a great many sexologists that
all preferences, including sexual ones, are learned; for
which reason the expectations in particular cultures become critical in determining the fraction of people in
them who become heterosexual, homosexual, and bisexual.

According to psychoanalysis, the second element
often causative of homosexuality is *castration fear*. This
of course holds only for men. Because of castration
fear, the homosexual man is said to be withdrawing his
penis from the vagina. He fears that sexual intercourse
may castrate him. Psychoanalysts are sometimes in the
paradoxical position of saying that a homosexual man
has pulled his penis back from a vagina in fear, and then
has gone ahead and entrusted it to the mouths of
strangers, an act that would seem to the fearful even
more perilous than sexual intercourse.

The third main source of homosexuality, in the psychoanalytic view, is *narcissism*. One falls in love with
his own contour, like Narcissus, who supposedly fell
in love with his own image in the water. A narcissist is
someone who treats his own body "in the same way
as otherwise the body of a sexual object is treated."

In some cases, Freud said, the narcissist when admiring his own body, and perhaps caressing it, can find complete satisfaction. And, it was held by Freud and others, narcissism can lead to homosexuality where one's own body is replaced by that of another person of the same sex.

The fourth supposed cause of homosexuality in the Freudian scheme is *identification*. The person has identified too much with a member of the opposite sex, usually the parent, and has copied an erotic bent which he should not have copied. Usually, it is the boy growing up who supposedly has copied his mother too closely, and after incorporating her, comes to resemble her in his tastes as an adult. (The misconception that because a man feels sexual desire for men he must fancy himself a woman is still widespread.) Misplaced identification of this sort is said to be most apt to occur in boys whose mother is strong and domineering and whose father is weak, or for any reason does not spend time with the boy.

The theory that this configuration is apt to produce a homosexual son provides a strong argument for continuing with the conventional balance of power between man and wife. These days, as women are coming into their own, the balance of power is shifting toward equality. The theory that the combination of an assertive mother and weak father produces homosexual sons kills two birds with one stone. It points to the homosexual as a faulty product and it warns the woman seeking equality that she had better go slow, because if she becomes more assertive than her husband this may cause great harm to her children.

It need hardly be said that it is not enhancing to

think of oneself as having become homosexual because of castration fear, or narcissism, or fixation, or over-identification with a parent. In the psychoanalytic scheme there is no way to become homosexual unless it is due to failure of some sort. This has remained the psychoanalytic position. "All psychoanalytic theories assume that adult homosexuality is psychopathological and assign differing weights to constitutional and experiential determinants" (Bieber).

That psychoanalysts are still patterning in the conventional design for living brought to us by Christianity may be seen in the tendency to group homosexuality with other sex acts similarly condemned. The underlying similarity is that these other acts are not reproductive either; their only explicable aim can be the pursuit of pleasure. In Washington, D.C., a local psychiatrist named John R. Cavanagh gave a speech as part of a seminar on "Theology and Homosexuality" in November 1970. In talking about heterosexuals, Dr. Cavanagh said, "In some cases the manifestation of homosexuality may be, for example, a perverse form of sexual intercourse, such as fellatio or sodomy." Cavanagh thus used psychoanalytic theory, as the notion of sin has often been used, to condemn "the perversions," even between man and wife, by describing them as disguised forms of homosexual expression. The assumption that everyone's ideal form of sexual expression should be the same, which is implicit in the idea of perversion, is repeatedly underscored in psychoanalysis.

Some of the currently used psychoanalytic techniques for maneuvering with homosexuals during the actual sessions are conveyed to us by Lawrence Hatterer, M.D., who reports actual dialogue. The single most powerful method of discouragement of an activity, invented by psychoanalysts, is the demand that the person explore its motivations and understand them fully before doing what he wants to do, or even trying it out for a period. The analyst can pursue his inquiry wherever he wants, and thus if the patient is "well motivated for cure" the analyst can easily impart the idea that the patient had incomplete understanding of his homosexual urges, when the truth is that the same inquiry could be leveled at heterosexuals too and would reveal the same inability to keep producing explanations.

Consider this dialogue between Dr. Hatterer and one of his patients.

PATIENT: The point is that just about every time I see a magazine, I start flipping pages and want to look at men.

THERAPIST: Do you understand why?

PATIENT: That would probably be the very root of the problem.

THERAPIST: Why?

PATIENT: I mean, if I knew why I was looking at it, I'd be better.

THERAPIST: It's just what we've got to explore.

If the word "women" replaced "men" in the patient's first statement, and the question were the same, the difficulty in producing explanations for the behavior would have been as quickly revealed. But doubtless, the same question would not have been asked, since the "why" question is an attempt to dislodge behavior that is unwanted by the therapist, and often by the

patient. On the cover of Hatterer's book, he is credited
with having worked for over fifteen years with patients
"troubled and untroubled by a vast spectrum of homosexual fantasy, impulse, act and milieu." If the patient
is not troubled at the outset, persistent questions about
the origin of his homosexual urges are almost sure to
arouse misgivings, especially since the patient's life
must be going badly for him or he would not have come
for help of any kind.

The psychoanalyst, by stressing the importance of
understanding the origin of the homosexuality, conveys
the idea that the inquiry itself should be a prerequisite
for pursuing a homosexual life. Inquiry is often in-
structive and interesting. But on the assumption that
life is short, individuals must learn to weigh their personal decisions chiefly by the consequences envisioned
as outcomes of the different choices possible for them.
These consequences naturally involve humanistic and
ethical considerations, but the person acting must always remember his right to consider himself a proper
beneficiary of decisions he is to make. The very decision to arrest a trial-and-error process and to replace
it by inquiry is a decision about how life should be
lived.

The emphasis of psychoanalysis has always been on
examination as opposed to action. In the early days,
Freud and his disciples exacted from their patients an
agreement before treatment that during its course they
would not make major changes in their lives, like getting married, or quitting an important job. Some stick-
lers among psychoanalysts still make this demand.

Dr. Thomas Szasz has likened psychoanalysts to
preachers. They are never more so than when arguing

for sexual abstinence. In his book *The Manufacture of Madness,* Dr. Szasz illustrates this with one case after another from the psychoanalytic records. Karl Menninger, a supposedly progressive psychoanalytic spokesman, advised a homosexual man to live continently. Szasz, in *The Manufacture of Madness,* describes the psychiatric view of homosexuality as "a thinly disguised replica of the religious perspective which it displaced." Of Menninger's psychoanalytic advice to the homosexual man, Szasz writes that it "bears out the suspicion that his medical role is but a cloak for that of the moralist and social engineer."

To help convince the homosexual patient that he ought to change, psychoanalysts use the device of accounting for whatever difficulties he presents in terms of the homosexuality. The inability to get along with people, difficulties with authorities, with members of the opposite sex, even the inability to do creative work, have all been blamed on homosexuality at different times by psychoanalysts. Doing this is extremely demoralizing to patients, and turns them away from discoverable solutions. Instead of increasing the person's understanding of how he offends people or prevents himself from working, the analyst preoccupies him with thinking about his homosexuality and how it might be harming him.

Even where the patient's despondency is an obvious reaction to a recent failure in a nonsexual realm, Hatterer stands ready to use it as evidence that the person has chosen the wrong sexual course. In trying to effect change, psychoanalysts are not averse to marshalling misgivings from any source. Hatterer advises supporting "the patient's past or present religious values which are incompatible with his homosexuality." He says not to stress the punitive or "guilt-oriented" part of religion, but instead the patient's "ethics" and his "need to live an integrated existence."

In place of the Hell used by preachers to frighten homosexuals, psychoanalysis warns homosexuals that they will suffer a dissolute life, an incomplete existence, an old age spent in misery. Hatterer explains in detail how he convinces patients of this.

For instance, take a statement like "I've stopped looking for my Prince Charming. He doesn't exist." Hatterer says that such an assertion indicates the patient's "own wish to change." When this happens, he says, the therapist can "further reinforce the patient's feeling that a 'homosexual marriage' is futile by offering his observations of homosexual marriages based on his clinical experience."

Here is one such commentary by Hatterer, made to a patient:

> Most of these relationships are precarious and needless to say, I've seen some very destroyed human beings who have felt the ravages of attempts to sustain a permanent homosexual relationship. Much of what you've said now and before shows that you have stunning insights into the whole scene and what is and is not possible.

And watch how Hatterer changes the subject sharply after the patient speaks, in this next piece of dialogue:

> PATIENT: I was moderately interested in her, not very interested at first, she's not that attractive. Well, I would say for the rest of the evening she kept coming back, and particularly after she'd had more to drink she became somewhat more friendly and asked me

to her cottage the next day. What I don't understand is when I came into the city from the beach, I felt more homosexual than less on Sunday night.

HATTERER: Has she been the one to initiate or keep up the contact with you, or have you been calling her?

In the same session, the patient mentioned heterosexual feelings, and Hatterer rejoiced in them as coin of the realm.

PATIENT: I thought that you'd be pleased to hear that I've gotten rolling and in the past few weeks something's happening with me and Donna, the girl I told you about.

HATTERER: Wonderful! What's been happening? Donna is the first girl you've had genuine strong feelings for and been able to express them.

These days it is standard practice for psychoanalysts to use their presumed authority to reinforce what they consider good behavior by dwelling on it and showing their admiration. The combination of playing down the homosexual side and playing up the heterosexual one would never have been used by Freud. For the psychoanalyst to convey his opinions loudly during a session is still considered poor analysis by rigorous Freudians. The whole art of analysis, in their view, is to elicit the patient's own, pure, private predilection for viewing people. What the patient brings is the stuff of the analysis. This is the classical Freudian view, and according to it, the analyst must step back, and not offer opinions.

There are thousands of articles on homosexuality in psychoanalytic literature. Few if any talk of helping homosexual men or women overcome their conflicts over the life they chose. One would not expect them to. Most psychoanalytic training institutes, like most training programs in psychology, would refuse a declared homosexual as a trainee. Therapists of all schools are still authenticating themselves by treating homosexuality as a problem.

What the public finds revolting is almost sure to be called neurotic by the psychoanalyst, and psychoanalysts exert far more influence on public opinion than other therapists do. In March, 1971, Dr. Hatterer told a New York *Post* reporter, "This society is no more going to institutionalize homosexuality than we're going to institutionalize Al Capone" (March 11, "Daily Closeup"). The official psychoanalytic position becomes a misfortune for the person who goes to a practitioner in the hope of getting a fresh view of his condition, or of his possibilities for happiness. One need not conform to a national stereotype of preferred behavior to be happy in a culture as diverse as ours.

As Szasz points out, both the law and public opinion look to psychiatric opinion for justification. He describes how even court judges "like to transform moral problems into medical or psychological ones; they prefer to do 'the right thing' medically, or psychologically, rather than morally." Thus not only do so-called mental health experts rely on conventional values, but their word becomes an authentication of beliefs. When a psychologist testified a few years ago at a nationally publicized murder trial that epilepsy existed and might have been a contributing cause, he was providing a rationale for the already widespread belief that epileptics are hideous and to be feared. Mental health workers take their cues from both public attitudes and the law, and give their seal of approval to both.

Not till there is general sympathy will psychologists and others give homosexuals their seal of approval. When enough homosexuals have come forth and cured the public of its phobic fear of homosexuals, psychologists as a group will doubtless allow that at least some homosexuals are healthy. And they may even render a service when this happens.

At one time public opinion was appalled at masturbation. Technically it was against the law, and topflight psychologists and medical doctors believed it was both depraved and harmful. Now that the public has won its right to masturbate without guilt, psychologists grant them that right. In fact, as we shall see, psychologists even utilize the new open attitude toward masturbation sometimes, by getting patients to masturbate as part of a therapy procedure. As the prevailing attitude toward masturbation changed (due more to Kinsey's work than all other influences combined), mental health workers were changing their minds too; in the end, the writings of psychologists hastened the enlightenment. Psychologists themselves were often cited as mental health experts who said it was all right to masturbate. People who had gone ahead without permission felt vindicated. Their eyesight, or sanity, or whatever else was said to be endangered, must have seemed like new again.

The day may come when prevailing psychiatric opinion will be that homosexuals are not all sick men and women. But it is not advisable for homosexuals to wait

for this. Always it remains up to the individual to decide for himself which experts are to be followed, and
how far.

Not just psychoanalysts but therapists of all schools
who hold fixed ideas about homosexuals are contributing to the maintenance of their own ideas without
knowing it. By the time these people come to meet homosexual men and women as colleagues, their attitudes
toward homosexuals are already known. The person is
then careful not to reveal that he or she is homosexual.
The practitioner thus goes on believing that all homosexual men and women are unhappy, and even feels
legitimate in using his own experience in making this
case to the patient.

I once sat in a restaurant with a world-famous psychoanalyst and a gay friend of his who had brought me
to meet him. The psychoanalyst didn't know his friend
was gay. After talking about Freud nostalgically, he
asked the person warmly about his life plans, and inquired as to whether there were new developments in
his personal life. Though the psychoanalyst obviously
liked the young man, then a budding psychiatrist, there
was never a mention by the man that he was homosexual and had just invested his life savings in buying a
house with his lover. There isn't much future in de-
claring yourself to a person convinced that all homosexuals are "neurotic" or "maladaptive." Not surpris-
ingly, the psychiatrist remained silent on the topic of
his homosexuality. And thus the psychoanalyst, even
if he would have been open to a new view of homosexuals, never got the chance to know that this person,
whom he respected, and whose life seemed to be run-

ning smoothly, was homosexual. As a result, the psychoanalyst was deprived of information, primarily because he was distinguished in his field and his views on homosexuality were known.

Almost the same thing happened in connection with a leading behavioral therapist. Recently, a colleague of mine marched into my office and plunked down on my desk a sheet of paper this therapist had handed out to a group of psychiatrists in Pennsylvania. It specified rules for punishment to be followed as part of a technique for treating homosexuals. The person who came into my office this time was also homosexual—a woman who had overcome her conflicts about it many years earlier. She was infuriated over the list of rules. She had spent a year working under the close supervision of the behavior therapist but had not spoken up. Her case was like the earlier one. She had wanted to learn the therapist's system of treatment and then to select what seemed valuable, and the best way to do that seemed to be not to rock the boat. At no time did it seem indicated to tell the distinguished therapist that she was homosexual. A possible advantage would have been the encouragement of him to regard his homosexual patients differently. But, in her opinion, the chance of this seemed too slight to warrant the exposure. Perhaps she was right. Who knows? The trouble is that regardless of how individual experts would respond if all the homosexuals among their acquaintances declared themselves, this tends not to happen.

Consider the following passage, which suggests a second reason why the prejudice persists in professional groups. Its vagueness makes it hard to pick up and remove:

> Whereas the ordinary phobic patient knows that he is suffering from specific fears, no matter how effectively he may deny or belittle their importance, the homosexual complains—if at all—only of feeling sexually indifferent to women. The unconscious anxieties are effectively hidden by an attitude of superiority or hate in some cases, and in others by an exceptional ease in social contacts with women, varying from friendly identification to marked ingratiation. (Rubenstein)

The comment is like a net, and there is no escape from it once a person says he is homosexual. There is no possible way for a homosexual man to argue his case, no possible life he could lead or point to, that would demand reconsideration of homosexuality by the psychoanalyst who made the statement. Even "exceptional ease in social contacts with women" falls into the category of being a defense helping the person to bury his "unconscious anxieties." Psychoanalytic theory is riddled with such assertions. They are framed in such a way that they can never be disproven by evidence.

The psychoanalyst Irving Bieber assumed at the outset of a research survey reported in 1964 "that homosexuality is psychopathologic." He then chose psychiatrically disturbed patients in treatment as his sample for study, and used forms filled out by their psychoanalysts as the measure of how they had changed. At the end of the ten-year project he concluded that he had been right in his original assumptions.

Bieber is perhaps an extreme. Once he even wrote that bachelorhood is symptomatic of psychopathology. A superb evaluation of the Bieber study was done by Dr. Fritz Fluckiger, who called his monograph "Research Through a Glass Darkly." Also Dr. Wainwright Churchill listed numerous glaring faults in the Bieber report.

Especially in the last twenty years, psychoanalysis has been widely disparaged. Analysts themselves have become a natural subject for caricature. But this is because too much credence was given to Freud and his disciples in the first place. Playwrights, novelists and historians had taken some of the premises of psychoanalysis as if they were basic truths, needing no demonstration. For a time people imagined that they could accomplish personal change by paying for insights. Not just the time and money, but the idolatry and suspension of disbelief given to "one's analyst" were too much for anyone. Many people in the analyst's office have impotently tried to discharge their rage, caused by everyday frustration, by railing against their parents, only to feel the same rage, caused by frustration from the same basic problems, years afterwards.

Disillusionment with formal psychoanalysis is growing. In most such cases, if the psychoanalytic patients instead of spending years on the couch, had been looking for their own self-defeating activities, they would be much better off. These days relatively few persons contemplating treatment are willing to go for classical psychoanalysis, four or five times a week. And since nearly everyone with a new therapy method, and many people without one, have been taking pot shots at

Freud, there isn't sufficient faith left either, to sustain more than a small number of traditional psychoanalysts. More than a few of our leading nonfiction writers have made their reputations disparaging Freud, and the barrage has taken its toll.

Still, one feels that Freud was more humane than to settle for his patient's living a pleasureless life, accomplished by his giving up his homosexuality. On the basis of his inability to accomplish true conversion, he despaired of the success of his method as applied to homosexuals. In his essay on homosexuality in women, he wrote, "To try to convert a developed homosexual is hardly more promising than to try the reverse, only that for good, practical reasons, the latter is never attempted." And late in his life, he wrote to the mother of a homosexual boy that she should not expect analysis to eliminate his homosexuality. "What analysis can do for your son runs in a different line. If he is unhappy, neurotic, torn by conflicts, inhibited in his social life, analysis may bring him harmony, peace of mind, full efficiency, whether he remains a homosexual or gets changed."

This now famous letter, by the way, was not in the Freudian archives till Kinsey received it from the mother. On a whim she had sent it off with a note to Kinsey saying that he would perhaps be interested in it, since the conclusions he had reached in his first volume on sex behavior resembled Freud's.

For a time I thought I understood why the typical psychoanalyst is dogmatic and conventional about homosexuals. He had never known a homosexual except those who went to him for help, so naturally he thought they were all incapacitated and wanted to change. As I went down the list, I saw that none of my psychoanalyst acquaintances had homosexuals as intimate friends (except of course for those who were themselves homosexuals, and they were a tiny minority). To convince the typical psychoanalyst that even one happy and productive homosexual existed, it seemed to me, would be to defeat the argument that homosexuals are necessarily incompetent, dangerous and discontented. And so, naively, I arranged to juxtapose members of these two groups in the confines of my living room. Following the practice of Kinsey, who, I had heard, once tried a similar experiment, I chose genial and well-informed homosexuals, whose professional and personal lives were above any sort of reproach I could think of.

But my experiment failed, and badly at that. The psychoanalysts were unduly and inhumanly polite all evening. No matter how well the dinners went, afterwards they would make specific complaints about the homosexuals, or say nothing but make clear they wanted no more contact with them. Though I fought against the conclusion, since several of the psychoanalysts were close friends of mine, I could not escape it: Once an attitude is formed, in some cases at least, it may not be dislodged by evidence alone. Or, since I am talking about distinguished professionals, here it is appropriate to say: You can lead an expert to the source of his fear and disgust, but you cannot always make him drink of his observations.

THREE

THE CASE AGAINST
TRYING TO CONVERT

The majority of therapists of nearly all schools, and
not just psychoanalysts, view homosexuality as an illness. To most, it is a special kind of illness, one too
distressing to be looked at in close detail. Unlike certain researchers—for instance, Dr. Evelyn Hooker—
therapists do not seek out homosexuals who are happy
in order to study their lives. Nor do their writings indicate any learning about the lives of homosexual men
or women which might be gotten from publications for
homosexuals, such as the newspapers *Gay* and *The
Advocate*. With the exception of occasional citations of
statistics from Kinsey, these therapists make few references to books by those who do not consider homosexuality an illness, such as Churchill, Hoffman and
Hooker. Perhaps these people feel it would be a waste

of time to study the thing they are trying to eradicate. At any rate, virtually the entirety of learning that goes into the development of new treatment methods comes from old ones that have failed.

Most therapists treat many more homosexual men than women, doubtless because their "problem" is considered more severe. Nearly all therapists bypass the direction pointed to by Kinsey as the one in which psychology ought to go, namely that it ought to aim at determining why some people can depart from group custom without suffering and others cannot. Moreover, though many of these nonpsychoanalytic therapists talk about using trial and error, it never occurs to any of them to do so around sexual preference. Anyone who has spent years trying an approach that has left him as miserable as before would be wise to try another. But those who work at converting homosexuals do not offer their services if the patient's aim is to learn to accept and enjoy his homosexuality. Nor do they allow the patient the option of considering various goals during treatments.

Havelock Ellis once wrote that "it is possible for a homosexual man to engage in sexual intercourse but not to fall in love with a woman." To the therapists treating people for homosexuality as if it were an illness, the question of falling in love heterosexually does not arise. Cure consists in getting the person to stop the homosexual behavior, even if he goes on yearning for it. There is never the consideration that they may be asking the patient to capitulate to a life without romantic love.

In addition, the experiments are riddled with failures

of scientific method. Outcomes are almost invariably decided on the basis of reports by patients, usually within a few months of treatment, and seldom after as long as two years. At the very least, such reports are in the form of testimony to a doctor who has been marshalling medicine, and embarrassment, in his push to get the patient to repudiate his homosexual life. Often, as we shall see, it is a report to a person who has done violence to the patient, and who stands ready to do more if the patient says he has not changed.

Let's look at a sample of the nonpsychoanalytic methods tried in the nineteen-sixties. From my point of view, they range from the zany to the gruesome. Two of them—brain surgery and emetic persuasion—make unpleasant reading. I include them as representatives of the category already branded by some as barely disguised methods of punishment. Opponents of so-called *aversive techniques,* methods that entail punishment, became vociferous for the first time in 1970, and homophile groups around the country are actively opposing the use of these techniques.

Naturally, any selection is arbitrary to some degree, but I think the reader who investigates further after reading this chapter will find that I have not chosen a biased sample.

Behavioral Therapy

The psychiatrist Joseph Wolpe, called a behavioral therapist, is responsible for a method widely used, called *systematic desensitization.* The premise is that one can't be anxious and relaxed at the same time. The situation causing homosexuality, or any supposed difficulty to be treated, is conceived of as on a gradient. Earlier steps are situations of the sort that cause problems of lesser severity, ranging in difficulty up to and including the actual problem situation itself. The situations are considered as rungs on a psychic ladder.

The first step is to get the patient to imagine he is on the first rung, and to be sure that he is relaxed while contemplating himself there. His relaxation may be induced either by a barbiturate, as in the case to be discussed, or by having the patient employ a method of relaxation he is taught for the purpose. Either way, so long as the patient is able to relax while undergoing each experience on the gradient.

As he is able to do this on each rung, he goes on to the next, and so forth. He may undergo each experience vicariously, by imagining it in the therapist's office; or, as part of a method used somewhat less often, he may subject himself to successively more difficult experiences out in the real world. In this case he is most usually asked to employ the method of relaxation he is taught, and does not use a barbiturate.

Very likely, the method works with some kinds of difficulties, where the essential problem is fear. For instance, one could perhaps help certain people overcome their fear of interacting with homosexuals by the method. But homosexual desires are not simply attributable to anxiety, and thus the method is inapplicable. There is more to cultivating heterosexual arousal than getting a person to take it easy.

In 1967, a characteristic attempt to treat homosexuality by the method of relaxation was undertaken by Dr. Tom Kraft in London. He wrote:

The use of systematic desensitization in the present study is based on the assumption that when a patient is desensitized from anxiety relating to normal sexual intercourse, he loses his homosexual desires, without any specific treatment being directed toward his homosexuality.

Disbelieving that homosexuals really enjoy their sexual acts, Dr. Kraft tried to treat a thirty-two-year-old man who had been homosexual since childhood, even during a brief marriage nine years earlier to a woman named Sarah. Here is a list of the experiences in the order that Dr. Kraft had the man envision them:

1. Talking to his former wife, Sarah
2. Kissing Sarah
3. Having Sarah sit on his lap
4. Embracing Sarah
5. Being in the bedroom with Sarah
6. Being in bed with Sarah
7. Kissing her goodnight in bed
8. Preliminary sex play
9. Sexual intercourse

Kraft thought his patient was progressing well, according to his report, but unexpectedly during the treatment, which was conducted in a hospital, the patient was discovered in mutual exposure with another male patient. Kraft wrote that "The therapist strongly discouraged this, and the patient has had no further interest in homosexual activities."

After whatever Dr. Kraft said to the patient, the homosexual behavior was not seen again, and nine months later the patient was pronounced cured. Kraft prided himself on having used only the method of "systematic desensitization," but of course his strong discouragement must be considered a factor, since in fact it was the turning point. In any event, nine months seems too short a time for us to conclude that this man, who was reportedly homosexual since childhood, has been converted. Dr. Wolpe himself has treated patients for homosexuality who reverted to it as much as two years after treatment was finished. In fairness to Dr. Wolpe, he did not design the method of "systematic desensitization" for use with homosexuals and he himself has tended to use it to change other sorts of conditions where it has fared much better.

Systematic desensitization is one of many methods used by the behavior therapists, a new group that sprang up in the sixties and that is still gaining adherents. The distinguishing features of this group are that they try to use verifiable definitions, keep speculation to a minimum, and so far as is possible base their techniques on principles already shown to hold psychologically. Since the behavior theorists insist on strict criteria before accepting that a principle has been demonstrated, this last requirement leads to a frequent insistence that the principles have been shown in the laboratory for lower organisms. In the words of the best known of the behavior therapists, the psychologist H. J. Eysenck, "Behavior therapy may be defined as the attempt to alter human behavior and emotion in a beneficial manner according to the laws of modern learning theory."

The behavior therapist always knows the precise outcome that constitutes success for him. He does not encourage trial and error. The assumption is that he knows how the patient ought to change. Often making this decision is easy, as when a person wants to get rid of headaches. But not when there are roads still to be explored before the decision is made. From what I have been able to ascertain after reading many books and hundreds of articles on behavior therapy, the decision is always to help the patient move in the direction of being like the majority, where this becomes an issue. There is perhaps no case in the literature in which a behavior therapist helped a homosexual patient to recover from guilt.

In the words of the writer of one of the best-known textbooks on behavior therapy, Aubrey Yates, "Behavior therapy deals with abnormalities of behavior, whether these behaviors define neurotic or psychotic states, or whether they occur in essentially normal persons."

With their scientific headstart, behavior therapists could conceivably have thrown light on how homosexuality develops. It exists virtually all through the animal kingdom, and one might have expected them to study it there. But perhaps even more readily than the Freudians, the behavior therapists accept tenets of social convention as dictates on what will make people happy, and they show no signs of re-examining them. Time and again, they give these tenets scientific status alongside the most thoroughly verified of their psychological principles. Because they impose on one patient after another their stamp of what they think ought to be, they do virtually no learning about new life-styles. They readily admit that if customs were different, their aims with patients would differ, and though this is perhaps true to some degree of all therapists, it is a blind truth with them. Patients who would do best by not conforming are not given the chance to discover this by the behavior therapists.

We have already seen an example of how behavioral theory is bounded by conformity, in the case presented. The assumption made by Dr. Kraft that his homosexual patient must have gotten that way in response to anxiety is a totally unwarranted view. The personal histories of most homosexual men supply no reason for believing that fear of sexual contact with women drove them to their choice. Nothing intrinsic to behavior theory demands this conclusion. In fact, in other contexts, the behavioral therapists argue, quite correctly, that there are many ways to learn any preference. From this it would allow that the reinforcements for homosexuality might as easily have been good experiences in homosexual contacts as bad experiences in heterosexual ones. The assumption that bad experiences must have driven the person to homosexuality was for a time made by Freud, and has been popular folklore. Behind it is the belief that no one would choose so unconventional a life-course unless he were afraid to pursue the conventional one.

The behavioral therapists make no bones about feeling qualified to judge for people what is good for them. They assume that everyone has as his primary purpose to live up to easily identifiable social expectations. Perhaps most people would like to be socially well-esteemed, but they would like other things too; and one of the reasons a person used to go to a psychologist was to find out what he wanted and what would make him happy. In the behavioral scheme, the best result is always obtained by making the best adaptation to one's society:

The person whose behavior is maladaptive does not fully live up to the expectations for one in his role, does not respond to all the stimuli actually present, and does not attain the typical or maximum forms of reinforcement available to one of his status. . . . Behavior that one culture might consider maladaptive . . . is adaptive in another culture if the person so behaving is responding to all the cues present in the situation in a manner likely to lead to his obtaining reinforcement appropriate to his status in the society. (Ullman and Krasner)

Presumably, the behavioral therapists themselves are to decide whether each of us is "fully living up to the expectations for one in his role." And what about the phrase, "respond to all the stimuli actually present"? The experts have decided, on the basis of what they were taught as children, that members of one's own sex are not to be included among these stimuli. If sometime in the future, homosexuality becomes acceptable socially, the behavioral therapists will accept it as no longer being maladaptive. Meanwhile these therapists are, as a group, punishing homosexuals and not considering their case. Moreover, by default, they are taken as qualified experts who have studied homosexuality and found it a condition needing treatment.

Dr. Wolpe has defined neurotic behavior as "any persistent acquired habit of unadaptive behavior." According to him, anxiety has usually been present in the situation that caused unadaptive behavior. Since by his definition, homosexuality is unadaptive, it would seem that without gathering evidence, he has defined homosexuality as originating in anxiety. In effect, he is saying, "If you aren't seeking your satisfactions as

I would expect you to, then you are on the wrong track, and you must have gotten on that track by being anxious."

This was the logic that led to the application of the systematic-desensitization technique to homosexuality. Upon the basis of no evidence, except their own incredulousness that someone would act in as unpopular a way as the homosexual does, behavior therapists have been trying to lure homosexual patients back toward heterosexuality—supposedly the long-lost Eden for them, "the maximum form of reinforcement available."

It is not surprising that this method, and others tried by the behavioral therapists, have been failures. Erotic feelings cannot be induced in homosexuals simply by enabling them to feel utterly relaxed while juxtaposed, naked, on a bed with a member of the opposite sex. Perhaps one can learn to go through the motions that way, and the pleasure of this accomplishment may last for a while. However, such performances, even if characterized as "satisfactory" by a behavior therapist, are unlikely to be worth much, and certainly cannot supplant an erotic preference that has been motivating a life outlook for years. Especially where the person has greatly enjoyed homosexual contacts, he is certain to feel a world of difference between them and heterosexual ones.

Moral Persuasion

In 1962 a method was attempted which caught on for a while. It can best be described as *moral persuasion;* modified forms of it are still being carried out in conjunction with other methods. Dr. Basil James, best-known early proponent of it, must have appeared to his patient very much like a frantic father at the end of his rope with his homosexual son. The doctor ranged from quiet explanations to reproducing the sound of vomit on a tape recording, all to make his point that homosexuality is bad.

In this study the persuasion was tried after giving the patient the emetic, apomorphine. As part of the treatment, one night

the patient was awakened every two hours and a record played which was frankly congratulatory and which explained in optimistic terms what would have been accomplished if, in fact, his homosexual drive had been reversed. At this stage no other treatment was given and next morning the patient was allowed up and about. On each of the third, fourth, and fifth days after the apomorphine treatment had finished a card was placed in his room, pasted on to it being carefully selected photographs of sexually attractive young women. Each morning he was given an injection of testosterone propionate and told to retire to his room when he felt any sexual excitement. He was provided with a record-player and records of a female vocalist whose performance is generally recognized as "sexy."

Since the follow-up study was done only months after treatment terminated, no convincing report of the outcome is available. One can imagine a great historian of the future describing persons like this one as having been crushed by the ignorant lawmakers and doctors of his day. But even now, there are hundreds of thousands of men and women not distressed by their homosexuality, and not viewing themselves as sinners; and thus the case could be made about any of these patients that he was less a victim of societal forces than of his own conventionality. In this view, the person was a victim of his overwhelming need to be told he was good by those he considered the authorities. In the end, one must decide whether a society is good that would restrict sexual behavior behind closed doors. The individual must decide to what extent he will honor restrictions, and whether honoring them is a help or a hindrance to him in giving his best to other people.

The Masturbation Method

In 1963, three doctors (Thorpe, Schmidt and Castell) devised a procedure which involved getting the patient to masturbate in the dark, while looking at pictures of a woman scantily dressed. Just before reaching orgasm he was instructed to inform the therapist in the next room. At this moment, the therapist would hit a switch that illuminated one of the pictures. It was hoped in this way to get him to associate the female form with his erotic feelings.

The patient did not prove a conquering hero:

Eight months after discharge, the patient wrote to say that he had been prevented from putting into practice his new found heterosexuality for two months after leaving hospital because he could not get rid of the person to whom he had sub-let his flat.

The notes go on to say he had attempted intercourse with one woman, who was "a virgin, nervous and unsatisfactory." The next sentence I find very important:

[He] had decided to wait until he would meet the right girl and fall in love.

Poor Miss Right! Often in such cases, the courtship is whirlwind; neither party has time to wait. The girl has wanted marriage, and the man has too, hoping it would help him. I have met a hundred women whose lives were seriously altered for the worse by their marrying homosexual men, often on the device of therapists who imagined the experience would be good for their patients.

The adult who feels strongly attracted to members of his own sex, has enjoyed sex contacts with them, and feels no attraction to members of the opposite sex after ample opportunity, should be very suspicious of the decision to wait till the right person of the opposite sex comes along. The right person may be a member of the same sex.

Brain Surgery

The *Medical World News* of September twenty-fifth, 1970, ran a story on Dr. Fritz Roeder called "Homosexuality Burned Out." Dr. Roeder "pinpoints" a section in the hypothalamus "that occupies less than a cubic centimeter of neural matter." Once it is located, he destroys it "with a series of tiny electrical burns."

"The reported result: Young homosexual men, most of them pedophiliacs, are promptly transformed into the straight world."

Dr. Roeder believes "that homosexuality is a sad pathologic upshot of faulty brain programming, often due to a severe androgen deficiency in early infancy."

When no lack of androgen was discovered in his own patients, Dr. Roeder resorted to the premise that there must have been one in the past. Dr. Roeder shares with most therapists who treat homosexuals the courage to act on his opinions.

Dr. Roeder's surgical assault on the hypothalamus compares with the old practice of prefrontal lobotomy. Neither could produce change in sex orientation, though either method of destroying brain matter might do away with the potential for sexual pleasure entirely, and could terminate the person's possibility for vivid fantasy. In one evaluation of lobotomies fifteen out of seventeen patients reported decreased vividness of fantasy. A characteristic report on a patient: "After operation, he continued to masturbate but fantasies were absent, and the autoerotic practice was simply to relieve tension."

Dr. Roeder announced that he had already done surgery on transvestites, exhibitionists, and just plain homosexuals, and according to him, with excellent success in stopping their deviant behavior. Since his criterion contains the idea of turning his surgical patients into "tractable human beings," it does not seem a stretch to liken his operation to the prefrontal lobotomy in its intentions or its effects.

The capacity for fantasy may not be especially important to Dr. Roeder or those who did lobotomies in the past. But some people *like* the idea of having a vivid imagination and would rather have some sexuality than none. The various surgeries for homosexuality illustrate more clearly than other forms of treatment what is being attempted for the most part. Swift justice, the redemption of an aberrant soul, that of the homosexual, the stifling of an activity and the destruction of the person's potential to enjoy that activity—with no other promises made to the patient, except that he will have less to fear from the law.

Emetic Persuasion

An emetic is a medicine or other substance that causes vomiting. The technique of using emetics to treat homosexuality and other forms of "deviancy" was very popular for a few years. It consists of giving the patient fetish objects, or showing him pictures of nude males, while rendering him acutely ill. Sometimes he is asked in advance to furnish the experimenter with pictures that arouse him sexually, ones that he has cut from a magazine, or snapshots he has taken of his lover. The scheme is to cause him dizziness and nausea which he will then associate with the photos or fetish objects.

Most commonly, apomorphine is injected intramuscularly. In England, a team that included a psychiatrist and a psychologist did therapy on a man every two hours for six days and six nights.

He received a total of 66 emetic trials, one every two hours, which consisted of: 53 intramuscular injections of apomorphine, one intramuscular injection of emetine hydrochloride, 5 oral doses of emetine hydrochloride in a tumbler of warm water, one dose of two dessertspoons full of mustard in a tumbler of warm water, 3 doses of 2 tablespoons full of salt in a tumbler of warm water, and three intramuscular injections of sterile water. . . . Dexamphetamine sulphate (5 mg) was given frequently to facilitate conditioning. . . .

The author of the paper describing this procedure, Dr. J. C. Barker, reported the patient's reactions in the British *Journal of Psychiatry* in 1965.

Vomiting invariably occurred in the earlier trials, but owing to drug tolerance it was either absent or replaced by headache, nausea and giddiness in the later ones. . . .

Lest we worry, Dr. Barker assures us:

The patient's physical condition remained excellent during the greater part of the treatment. He did not become dehydrated through repeated vomiting and insisted upon occupying himself as much as possible. His wife encouraged him on several visits during treatment, and he took part in animated discussions with his attendants between injections.

After the 68th trial, however, he exhibited rigors, a temperature of 99 degrees and an elevated blood pressure. He became hostile toward his attendants, appeared confused and was unable to maintain a normal conversation, and his co-ordination was impaired. It was considered that the cumulative effects of dexamphetamine were largely responsible for this rapid deterioration. He was given amylobarbitone sodium gr 6 and all these symptoms disappeared completely after a few hours sleep. (Barker)

Soon after treatment the patient left the country. Eighteen months after the treatment, Dr. Barker was able to write that "as far as is known, he remained symptom free." Barker proudly debunked a Freudian theory on the basis of his findings, though he does tell us that on one occasion after the treatment, the patient put on his wife's green skirt "which had formerly been a highly stimulating garment to him, but it produced no effects whatever."

Even so, Barker felt able to conclude that "recovery had been complete," because the man became "indifferent to wearing the garments which had previously excited him."

What harm had society in store for the poor victim comparable to the harm done to him? Even if it were shown that such treatment invariably eradicated the urge, one could question the ethics of administering it. But here there was much reason to suspect it would not work. No method has proven itself yet, and survived. In the same paper, Barker made a strong argument in favor of giving electric shock to patients as the punishing stimulus, instead of using emetics. In fact, he went so far as to present the design of an electric grid for the purpose. Since 1965, when the paper appeared, electric-shock conditioning has replaced emetic conditioning as the preferred "aversive method."

However, the situation is changing somewhat. Late in 1970 at the Biltmore Hotel in Los Angeles, the psychologist Dr. M. P. Feldman was giving a lecture to professionals on the use of electric-shock conditioning, when he was rudely interrupted. Members of the Gay Liberation Front in California and many others opposed to "aversive therapy" for homosexuals put on a mass demonstration. At first, they were refused the chance to speak, but hundreds demanded the right to have their view presented; this was that homosexuals suffer not because of neurosis but because of harassment.

According to *The Advocate,* published in Los Angeles, Dr. Feldman at first snatched his briefcase and hurried down the aisle as if he expected violence. However, he soon returned and, by the testimony of homophile leaders and the psychologists present, a discussion took place in which homosexuals for one of the first times were given the chance to speak for themselves. A few weeks later in New York City, a group of male orderlies who had been witness to aversive treatment of homosexuals in several hospitals banded together and put on a similar demonstration. Both demonstrations received newspaper coverage.

The use of aversive conditioning methods with so-called deviates has been opposed not just by homophile leaders but by many professional psychotherapists. Psychoanalysts as a group are opposed to them: The renowned Freudian psychoanalyst Edmund Glover, M.D., has fulminated against them. In describing the use of punishment and suggestion, Glover wrote

> It has the same penal significance which lies behind the application of the death penalty for murder, the therapeutic difference being that the latter conditioning process extinguishes the patient as well as his unadapted synaptic responses.

Homosexuals Anonymous

There's a new organization called "Homosexuals Anonymous." "Cured" homosexuals will meet in groups a few times a week. And if one of the "cured" feels unexpectedly overwrought with homosexual urges some night, he will be able to call up another "cured" person who will rush to his home to be with him. This way the "cured" will supposedly reinforce their cures, by underscoring each other's guilt in little speeches. And eventually, it is planned, the group may even do rescue work in homosexual hangouts.

The psychologists in New York and Philadelphia who are just beginning to assemble these groups, have the virtue of having admitted implicitly that homosexuality is "incurable." Their plan could make sense only if its premise were that the members had not been permanently cured, and continued to need each other's support. "Once an alcoholic, always an alcoholic": this is a motto of the highly successful national group, Alcoholics Anonymous. I suggest that the motto of the new group should be: "Once a homosexual, always a homosexual."

The name of the group, Homosexuals Anonymous, should come as a surprise to no one. Most homosexual men and women have been striving for anonymity as it is.

Conventionality for Its Own Sake

If control of behavior is regarded by society as essential in certain cases for the good of society as a whole (as indeed seems to be the case), then at least that control should, as far as possible, be based on rational rather than irrational consideration. (Yates)

This comment suggests that attempts to convert homosexuals are part of a larger plan, to subordinate the individual for the good of society, using psychological principles. Dr. M. P. Feldman, the leader in efforts to convert homosexuals by aversive training, has not limited himself to working with homosexuals. He sometimes tries to bend heterosexual tastes toward conventionality too:

> For instance, one of our patients had a strong degree of sexual interest in women much older than himself and only a small degree of interest in females of his own age. Treatment of him consisted of a modification of the anticipatory avoidance learning technique described in connection with the treatment of homosexuality. His progress was recorded in much the same way as for our homosexual patients.

The relative ages of two adults who are motivated to enjoy each other sexually should properly be of concern to no one but local gossips, but even here the experts have shown themselves eager to interfere using their punishment techniques. Finally, consider this instance in which the treatment was conducted by another specialist in deviancy:

> The patient was a 32-year-old bachelor who was sexually aroused by women's buttocks and bloomers. He had never had intercourse but masturbated with fantasies concerning these fetishes. The patient was given five aversion conditioning sessions. Three stimulants were used: the patient's photographs of women wearing bloomers, visual images of women with attractive buttocks, visual images of bloomers. The electric shocks were administered with an induction coil and finger electrodes. (Rachman)

The man enjoyed little—"bloomers," "women wearing bloomers," and "women with attractive buttocks." He had sought help to procure more sexual fulfillment, not less. Behavior theory might have regarded his already present sources of pleasure as valuable in leading him toward other forms of sexual expression. That is often a tactic. However, here the therapist ruthlessly set out to deprive the patient of his sole enjoyments, on the highly speculative thesis that doing so would benefit him.

Conclusion

To be convinced of the efficacy of any of the procedures mentioned, one would need to have seen success in studies with long follow-up periods. In actuality, when such research is done, the experimenter is hardly ever willing to wait more than some months, seldom as long as two years, before publishing his findings. And even within periods this short, it has been noted that patients revert. In spite of this, some therapists promise success to their patients, and many allow the patient to conclude that success will depend wholly upon the degree of his motivation to change.

So diversified are the methods tried that it is exceptional when as many as three different studies of the exact same procedure are reported. In fact, every method has its validity doubted by the overwhelming majority of practitioners. You might say that every therapist is doing his own thing, and in reports he mentions the research done by his predecessors only to indicate the place from which he departed.

Only some of the treatment methods use punishment as such; but the effect of trying to wipe out one's sexuality is always punishing. When a homosexual has sacrificed time and money to talk about the origins and ugliness of his homosexuality for years, and then finds himself unchanged, he has paid a price as costly in its way as that paid by the person who has been subjected to acute distress but for only a few months. Both are almost certain to dislike themselves more than ever for being homosexual, after the treatment.

I have gone over hundreds of studies done on attempts to convert homosexuals. Here I have not delved into the technical parts of those studies, the experimental design and the use of statistical methods. However, it should be added that the people doing this sort of work are far below psychologists as a group when it comes to insight into the tools of experimental design. As a research consultant and as author of a college statistics text for psychologists, I have had many research proposals cross my desk. Seldom have I seen any as slipshod as the general run of the work in this area.

One of the glaring faults has to do with "stopping time"—the amount of time designated as the follow-up period to be allowed before taking stock of outcomes. The stopping time should always be specified *before* an experiment is begun. The researcher must not have the continued option of determining when to consider his experiment over. With this privilege, one can wait if his patients are doing "poorly," and terminate his study when his findings look as good as they will ever look. Understandably, one is more eager to write things up when they look good than at other times. Also, the choice of which patients to report on when one has treated many patients is sometimes made by the therapist a year or two after treatment. This introduces a bias. One can treat hundreds of patients and report on a handful.

In a paper titled "Recovery from Sexual Deviations,"

Ian Stevenson and Joseph Wolpe have reported on treatment of three patients. One, a homosexual man, stopped for a time, had sexual relations with a woman, and got married. At the end of two years, however, he resumed homosexuality, having sexual relations with four different men. The authors accounted for this by saying that the man's wife had become ill for several months and that "during the abstinence this occasioned" he reverted. Then he stopped homosexuality again, and since the report was made after about three years, not two, his reaction to the treatment received a better report.

The obvious conclusion is that some degree of homosexual desire remained, and returned, at least intermittently. Even the most demoralized patients would consider treatment a failure if it did not remove the want. One would think that treatment would begin with patient and therapist discussing what they meant by cure. But there is virtually never such discussion. The authors use the word "recovery" in the title of their paper. But it is a rare homosexual who would undertake treatment if he knew in advance that two years after it was over he was to have four homosexual experiences.

The second patient of the three also reverted after treatment. But he too subsequently went a stretch of some years of exclusive heterosexuality. In this study, the experimenters' freedom to determine their stopping time introduced a bias. One must make explicit in advance of a study precisely when it will be considered terminated, just as one must decide in advance which patients will be included in the final tally. If one treats enough homosexuals, it is certain that some will go through periods of not engaging in homosexual acts. Just as one cannot choose those patients and report on them alone (which many researchers in this area have done), one cannot set the time for ending an experiment *after* knowing how the participants have performed.

The third patient treated and reported on by Wolpe and Stevenson was a heterosexual man, who had sexually molested small children. It is not unusual for homosexuals to be thrown together with this sort of sex offender, as if members of both groups were the same. It has been found that nonhomosexuals are more likely to molest children than homosexuals, but this finding is often disregarded. Also, when evaluating this research, it should be remembered, if fifty therapists plan to write up their findings, and two think they've converted homosexual patients, then most of the other forty-eight studies, if not all, will go unreported. Psychological literature shows mainly the arrows that appear to have hit the target, after incalculable arrows have been fired.

As for the aversive studies, it seems to me that the license of psychologists and others to go on doing them is expiring. There must come a time when it is decided that, since homosexuals cannot be honestly promised even a reasonable chance of conversion, they should be told the truth, that as a result of treatment they are apt to suffer more, not less.

Almost invariably, the rationale for these therapeutic assaults on homosexuality entails the belief that homosexuality is a shallow and superficial choice, one more readily subject to change than heterosexuality. Seldom do these therapists consider that even so specific an attachment as a fetish may have a broad base of motivations. They are utterly committed to the position that all so-called sex-deviancy is an isolated phenomenon. For instance, when trying to teach someone to despise his lover by getting the person to suffer at the sight of his lover's picture, it never occurs to them that they are sniping at a human relationship, as rich and full as their own love relationships, and in some cases richer. If it did, they would understand what they were tampering with, and would see their position realistically, as usually that of shooting a popgun at a battleship. They would understand that one walk in the countryside, one glorious Thanksgiving Day, one eager preparation to go away on a picnic together with a lover, might undo their work. They would see that one sad sniff of mortality shared with a lover, one rush to a veterinarian with a dog they both loved who died, if the patient had any judgment left, could undo the effects of the punishments inflicted by these masters, who in turn could offer much but could deliver little except loneliness and shame to the people they assulted.

Besides all this, the texture of one's fantasies and ambitions is so delicately woven that any attempt to rend it with a needle, to rip out some skein running through it, is an act of destruction. Many homosexuals entering therapy suffer the loss of what Alfred Adler called the person's "guiding fiction." Each of us has some dream, some seldom-if-ever-mentioned "airy ambition," which at best we accomplish only in part. The sort of ambition I am discussing nearly always involves friends or a lover or people we want to impress. If one is homosexual, unless the cultural fallout has filtered even the person's dreams, this highest yearning for intimacy will appear in the image of a love relationship with another homosexual. What could be simpler than this?

So the attack on one's sexuality, if one tries to convert, is a blow to intimacy.

A young man who had written successfully for television and wanted to be a playwright told me that during three years of psychoanalysis he was utterly unable to write. His dream was to turn out a Broadway hit, and to enjoy it on opening night with some imagined homosexual lover at his side. The magical moment would consist of his being called the most talented playwright on earth by his lover, and their leaving the theatre together. In real life, he had been hesitant in looking for the kind of lover he dreamed about; he did not like to think of himself as having a homosexual taste. Within the previous five years, he had been receiving more offers to write television scripts than he could handle, and he was a speedy writer. His financial success had enabled him to go to a psychoanalyst, something he had long wanted to do, been curious about.

Like many, this psychoanalyst believed that a homosexual orientation interferes with the creative process. There are famous cases of artists who were told, in no uncertain terms, that unless they changed they could not succeed. Such admonition was not given this time, but it was impressed upon him that his homosexuality sprang from illness—and this in itself was enough. In coming to despise his own guiding fiction, he drained off his motivation to write. In point of fact, he had not entered treatment to change his homosexuality, he said, but to discover ways to improve his already-excellent capacity to create. What he met was an assault on his very goal, the dream for which he had often toiled late into the night. Because the goal itself now seemed polluted, he stopped writing entirely.

He was my easiest patient to help, ever. My acceptance of what he cherished gave him hope almost immediately. In his case, the belief in the homosexual possibility gave him the sense that he need not be alone, that the work he produced might be seen and admired by an audience who would not hold his homosexuality against him. Observe that the prospect of an erotic love relationship with a homosexual was necessary. But as important was the sense that somewhere a community exists where he could be well-received if he accepted himself. The community of homosexuals had for him chiefly the value of being a population in which he would not be an outcast. Once he accepted himself as a homosexual, he was no longer alone—even though the only manifestation was that now he could labor alone for a time, and before he could not.

A guiding fiction in one form or another is the fuel each of us needs to exist alone. Without this fiction— our own idiosyncratic sense of what a hero is and what we must do to become one—our motive force is depleted. Who can say how much of our everyday life is touched by such dreams! I think a great deal.

By the time this book appears, there will doubtless be new techniques claiming success as cures of homosexuality. But the very fact that only a few years have elasped since a technique was invented means that the "cures" have been given insufficient time to prove their worth. Besides, the assumption that all homosexuals live wretched lives relieves those who work at trying to convert homosexuals from having to see how much damage they do in the process of treating them. Thus the picture of his prospects given to the homosexual patient who attempts to convert has been warped indeed.

FOUR

THE HEALTHY HOMOSEXUAL

MOTHER: You are doing this to hurt me.
LESBIAN DAUGHTER: That is egotistical. It has nothing to do with you.
MOTHER: But you might fall in love with a man.
LESBIAN DAUGHTER: Mother. No one asked you to consider the possibility that you might fall in love with a woman.

The young woman is assuming that her homosexuality needs no defense. This is why I would use the word "gay" to describe her.

For the remainder of this book and elsewhere, I propose a distinction between the words "homosexual" and "gay." To be homosexual is to have an erotic preference for members of one's own sex. One may be homosexual for a minute, an hour, a day, or a lifetime. The Kinsey scale measures degree of homosexuality or heterosexuality on a scale of from zero to six. Many people who write and talk on the subject are criticized for using the word "homosexual" without suggesting that there are degrees of homosexuality. This criticism is wrong. Kinsey used his scale to classify people by their behavior over a lifetime, but when people talk about themselves it makes perfect sense to think about one's recent past, or present desires. Kinsey was a genius as a surveyor and classifier. But for most purposes in everyday life, it makes sense to use the word "homosexual" to talk about people's present outlook. As Dr. Franklin Kameny put it some years ago, "Just as the heterosexual can abstain from sex completely and be no less a heterosexual for doing so, the homosexual can."

A homosexual person is gay when he regards himself as happily gifted with whatever capacity he has to see people as romantically beautiful. It is to be free of shame, guilt, regret over the fact that one is homosexual, that the searchlight of one's childhood vision of human beings shined more brilliantly on members of one's own sex than on those of the other. That, for whatever reasons, it illuminated those and gave them fascination—and burst them into sexual brilliance when the body learned to crave what it had been pursuing. To be gay is to view one's sexuality as the healthy heterosexual views his.

To be gay is to be free of the need for ongoing self-inquisition, the sort that preoccupies those who feel abandoned and are searching for a reason: "How did I become homosexual?" "Is it a disease?" "Who's to blame?" "Should I go for therapy?" "Was Julius Caesar homosexual?"

Being gay means having freed oneself of misgivings over being homosexual. At its best it means not limiting oneself to a stereotype—a model of some previous homosexual—for one's personality, at work, at parties, with a lover. It means remaining free to invent, to imbue life with fantasy. It means being able to investigate one's preferences and desires in sexual roles where one chooses, without having to construct a personality elsewhere consistent with this, to justify it, to account for it. In essence, it means being convinced that any erotic orientation and preference may be housed in any human being.

This implies that homosexuality in a man renders him no less masculine than other men, and that homosexuality in a woman makes her no less feminine. Curiously, the larger culture has decided that in men homosexuality connotes weakened sexuality, whereas in women it is a sign of enhanced sexuality. Lesbianism, belittled and misunderstood, has served as pornography for heterosexual men over the ages.

Many homosexuals have, when they discovered their orientation, begun acting in ways they believed consistent and necessary for their identity as homosexuals. For instance, they adopted highly defined masculine or feminine roles and elaborated upon them. Where one's whole personality becomes frozen in such a role, there is doubtless a reduction of possibility—a capitulation to a stereotype to escape conflict and to accept being homosexual. But suppose the person enjoys the role vigorously. Who is to say that the loss is disproportionate, or that the highest aim of life is total flexibility of role? Individuals must make these decisions for themselves.

Civilizations have often tried to cultivate what they considered a lush garden without weeds—a wholly heterosexual population. This has never been done. Unwanted, homosexuals have sprung up apparently nurtured by the same elements as heterosexuals. And in each population some of these homosexuals have boldly believed in themselves and their rights while others have accepted the conventional prejudice.

Some have never recognized a choice in the matter. Others have come to the great void of discovery unprepared, and have retreated. Society inculcated a fiction on them. It told them that only one vision of life was sensible—monogamous, heterosexual marriage with children. The removal of this fiction creates the void. By the retreat, I mean the flight from accepting that there are many vistas and each of us chooses his own.

What do we learn, sometime between the ages of five and fifteen, that seems to justify the merciless demand that we conform? If you asked the average five-year-old whether two adults should be permitted to touch each other's bodies and bring physical pleasure to each other if they choose, he would almost certainly say yes, provided he could understand the question. And if this is permissible for a man and a woman, why the outrage when it is a man and a man, or a woman and another woman? The child of five would be astounded if he understood that people were torn from their families and imprisoned for such acts.

And imagine if you told him that even as adults people were not permitted to wear on their own bodies what they pleased, that the state ruled on such matters too, that for wearing a dress in the street a man could be imprisoned and that his whole neighborhood would shrink back in horror.

The curious child might ask innocently what the person did wrong. If so, believers would perhaps be thankful that he had not asked instead with the same shining curiosity, "Whom did he harm?" To the child the questions might seem the same, and they should be considered identical in the moral realm; but as we grow up, we learn that society thinks of them as different, and as unrelated in many cases. The matter of right and wrong is often taught arbitrarily, said to be a matter of custom; and acts that harm no one are punished.

"What did he do wrong?" "Why child, he broke the law." To the detriment of all concerned, we are taught that this answer is satisfactory.

How are we taught this? What leads us to believe it? What does the child witness while growing up that makes it seem less of a shame, or no shame at all, when people are punished for harmless acts? Granted, the child's days are crammed with new experiences. But surely, he does not see harmless acts harming people.

On his way up the charted river of conventional living, the child learns revulsion. He learns from those around him when to feel disgusted, when to be outraged. And this learning becomes important; for as is well known, revulsion can fire the brain with violent convictions.

Chronic Self-Denial

The person who from early life has loathed himself for homosexual urges arrives at this attitude by a process exactly like the one occurring in heterosexuals who hold the prejudice against homosexuals. He votes against himself in everyday decisions—just as others vote against him. For instance, he may ridicule himself and other homosexuals, as prejudiced heterosexuals do. He desists from sexual contacts, as they would want him to. He reduces his career aspirations, as the heterosexuals would reduce them for him if they knew he was homosexual. He describes himself as sick, as heterosexuals would, and he direfully announces that all homosexual relationships must come to an unsavory end, in the very language used by heterosexuals who know nothing of such matters.

Like the prejudiced heterosexual, his early impressions about homosexuality came from the culture around him. As a child he has heard the same nasty references to homosexuals. He has heard them called "queers," seen them portrayed as dissolute and sad, on stage and screen, in novels, in newspaper articles. His own attitude toward homosexuality has evolved out of a context almost wholly derogatory. His prejudice against himself is an almost exact parallel to the prejudice against homosexuals held in the larger culture.

The issue of homosexuality is, of course, more urgent to him. In this case it is the issue of self. But the process by which he arrives at his adult estimation of homosexuality is explicable by the same basic principles. As with the learning of any attitude that becomes deep-seated, the earliest step is the forming of impressions. Next, by allowing those impressions to enter as a motivation for at least some decisions, and acting in accordance with them, the crucial step is taken of converting the impressions into heartfelt beliefs. Hearing laughter about homosexuals is receiving an impression. Deciding to laugh at homosexuals oneself gives seeming substance to the impression, makes it feel like one's own attitude. Having acted in any way on the basis of an impression, it becomes elevated in status and harder to dislodge. Every choice keeps alive the various beliefs that collectively motivated it. The choice to ridicule a homosexual man when the boys on the block are cracking jokes about him may have numerous motivations—the thought that the man may be grotesque, or may seem that way to others, and perhaps the desire to be liked by the gang. He welcomes the chance to scoff at the outsider, to feel and appear like an insider himself. If so, the single choice, though one of many made in the afternoon, would be adding to his conviction of the truth of all the implicit underlying beliefs. By even so simple an act, the boy would be making homosexuals seem ludicrous to himself, more so than before, and would be heightening his need to hold and express opinions that make him likeable.

By such acts, committed even before he discovers he is homosexual, he produces the contempt that he later comes to feel for himself.

I mention ridicule because, like liquor, it makes prejudices go down the hatch easily in the early stages. Ridicule is often the precursor to acts of violence. No matter that the victim is not damaged by it! Because its chief motive is contempt, there is a deepening of contempt for those ridiculed. This is in accordance with a critical principle accounting for the growth of all attitudes: Once a person acts on any belief—in this case, disdain for homosexuals—among the outcomes is that he makes the belief seem righter than ever.

This single principle is, I think, more important than any other in all of psychology. After holding numerous beliefs, we choose to act on certain of them, and by so doing we make them seem more reasonable. This occurs in accordance with a process which I have written about at length in *The Action Approach*. Our actions produce their own arguments. Our culture invites us to act in particular ways by holding up conspicuous rewards for certain kinds of actions and not others. After some trial and error, we arrive at highly individual methods of getting what we want, and then in striving for what we want, we create ourselves.

Especially early in life, attitudes tend to widen. Having elevated any attitude by basing decisions on it, we have made it seem more important to us; and next this attitude is apt to appear relevant to how we will handle ourselves in new contexts. It becomes a motive for still more activities, for a variety of new, habitual acts. Though the person acting never thinks of it this way, the new collection of activities is soon holding the attitude in place, so that it becomes harder to dislodge than it would have been shortly after it was learned. The widening process is more apt to occur early in life than later because in many more places we are still learning how to handle ourselves. Boys are taught to do a thousand things a week to emphasize that they are boys, not girls. Most are given to believe that homosexuality for them would connote girlishness, and thus the thought of harboring homosexual feelings becomes anathema. This does not happen all the time, of course. But it happens often. The dread of having homosexual feelings is learned even before there is a sense that many of the premises, such as that one will have a wife and children, are seen as threatened if one is homosexual. Perhaps fear of ridicule and ostracism, without any thought about why this would happen, is the chief motive for boys not wanting to be thought of as homosexuals.

The process of internalizing the cultural homophobia is different for women. Girls are not taught to shun boyishness with nearly such ferocity. Especially before the age of thirteen or so, many girls are allowed to dress like boys, play boys' games, and otherwise not to fear boyish identification. As I mentioned earlier, there is more tolerance when girls depart from their expected role than when boys do. The dread of being homosexual is not impressed upon girls as it is upon boys. One outcome of this is that girls tend to grow up with less fear of homosexuality in themselves and others. A second outcome is that girls, in part because they are allowed to act like boys, are much slower to discover their homosexuality, when it exists. Julie Lee, who answers many letters from troubled lesbians writing to her organization, The Daughters of Bilitis, in New York, tells me that a sizeable fraction came from women in their thirties who had first discovered that they were homosexual. Men seldom make this discovery in their thirties, and most make it in their teens. The boy who enjoys sewing is suspect at twelve, even if he is not homosexual. There is little a girl could do, short of discovering her own lesbian outlook, that would be taken as a sign of anything at that age. As a result of this slower awakening for women, which may be partly cultural and partly physiological, relatively more women than men are in the position of being married with children when they discover their homosexuality. Women are more apt to be faced with the problem of disentangling themselves and massively rearranging their lives, and great numbers of lesbians in this situation do nothing.

Flight into Guilt

The neurotic solution to the crisis of discovering that one is sexually unconventional is a flight into guilt. To understand the process well is the best way to resist succumbing to it.

A college boy who has known he was homosexual since age twelve has felt the usual conflicts over it. Because he does poorly on exams for the first time, a guidance counselor calls him in to ask what is the matter. He confesses that he is in love with another boy, and left himself too little time to study, and assures the counselor that he will do better the next semester.

The counselor sends him to a dean, who befriends him but announces firmly that his homosexuality is a sickness and that he can conquer it by exerting his will over it. The boy listens earnestly. He knows he is doing poorly in school. To heed this man of the world seems like a requisite for finding a remedy. The dean shows unusual patience in making sure the boy sees he is at a crossroads. He will either turn into a homosexual, or he will suppress the impulses, and in spite of all, make himself into the adult he once hoped to be. In so many words, the dean tells the boy he is on the verge of tossing away his whole future, everything he has been hoping for, as if it were a trifle.

The boy believes in the dichotomy as a complete statement of the possibilities before him. To believe the dean here is itself a choice of great importance. Not everyone would do this, and doubtless the boy's habitual attitude when knowledgeable elders give him advice is relevant to his decision here. To accept the choice as presented is to believe without further ado that a loved one is an enemy. Perhaps the boy feels some anxiety at this, but not enough to warn him of the dangers that lie ahead. He has always been an excellent scholar and a diligent worker. The dean is pleased but not surprised when the boy calls him the next day and tells him he has made the decision to give up being homosexual.

He decides to try. He is cool with his lover, and braces himself when the other boy cries pathetically. He quits membership in a club on campus, where there are many unembarrassed homosexuals. He makes it policy to avoid being with homosexuals permanently. He reads up on homosexuality under the heading of "deviancy" in his college library and undertakes to go to the school psychologist to nail down his conversion. All these acts, based on the premise that homosexual desires are anathema, heighten his loathing of the homosexual impulses he still feels. He is already dating girls, but experiences no erotic desires for any of them. This will come, he tells himself. He cannot help continuing to think that prowess with women is the real measure of manliness and of success.

He is once more a good student but more mechanical than before. He escorts girls to parties and to the theatre. He "succeeds" at sexual intercourse several times, but then his performance becomes uneven; and he worries about his sexual capability with women as he never did with men. He has not felt high romantic desire as a motive for any of this, but only the urgent wish to do the acceptable thing. In fact, more and more of his actions spring from conventionality. He is much more concerned with "doing the right thing" than a year ago, which puts a trace of primness in his presentation of himself. He finds himself most comfortable with girls who are timid, inexperienced.

One day, down the crowded corridor in college he sees a boy he once admired for his wit and humor. The boy, named Ted, seemed almost proud of being homosexual, was sprightly and animated, and seemed admirably unruffled by anything. Ted had recently said he was homosexual on a radio program, or so the boy had heard. Yet there seemed no way that his future would be marred. A lanky youth, he is blocking the hallway, talking to a handful of students, who are smiling. The boy stares at Ted, absorbed by his broad gestures as he speaks, though too far away to hear what he is saying. Then suddenly, he feels overcome with anger. And the vision comes to him of himself lunging toward Ted and choking him with both hands, pressing them into his throat to terminate his lively monologue and sink him to the marble floor. Ever since his own decision to change his style of life, he has thought of Ted as a living rebuke, and now he trembles at the sight of him. After glaring at him, he takes one symbolically aggressive step toward him, and then as if out of generosity, he turns fully around and walks in the other direction.

The flight into guilt always changes the homosexual's conception of who his friends and enemies are. By this time the boy no longer feels outrage at society for abuses against homosexuals, as he once did at moments, nor at the mental health experts who make public pronouncements that homosexuality always leads to misery. Such people are now seen as friendly. Has he not made major sacrifices already on the premise that this view is correct? These authorities are providing the justification for what he has done, and for this reason he depends upon them in moments of uncertainty, and feels deep respect for them. In the new configuration, they seem like sensible people whose theory assures him that he has made a wise choice.

Among those he once considered friends, many now seem like enemies. In particular, he regards as an enemy anyone who appears to be a mirror image of himself, because his enemy is himself. In his new life, he often senses he is being fraudulent, becomes bored. On dates, he looks at the clock and reminds himself to appear alert and to listen when spoken to. But time passes slowly, and sometimes he feels enraged at the people who welcome him in his present identity—as if they had put him in chains.

The flight into guilt is not only corrosive and fraudulent. It does not work. Anyone who belies the sensibleness of the great decision he is making is felt to be an enemy: satisfied homosexuals like Ted, who are not paying an obvious price for being homosexual; the occasional expert who says homosexuality is not an illness; the renowned novelist who is homosexual and outspoken about it, and who still seems to enjoy comfort and leisure and wealth.

In the days when he was trying to come to terms with being homosexual, and considered that society might be hostile, such people were like ports in a raging storm. They were the ones who, if he had told all to them in a great outpouring of honesty concerning how he felt and what he wanted, would have accepted him as he was. More than others, they were the ones capable of hearing out the details of his intimate feelings, and without censoring him, could have welcomed him as possessing an ability to love needing no correction. They could have come to his aid when the dean faced him with the great dichotomy, and offered him the counterexamples of their own lives. Now, feeling guilty, he shuns such people and their influences, and seeks solace among his real enemies—those who would not care if told that his exhilaration is gone, that he is superconventional and distrusts himself, and who will welcome him only as a heterosexual, which he is not.

The Healthy Outlook

How can the homosexual get rid of his or her internalized homophobia?

Because actions produce their own argument, there is no way to change an attitude except by disallowing it as a motive everywhere in one's life. This holds for prejudices as well as other attitudes of long standing. Often the actions are covert, whether the prejudice is against others or against the self. No one is hurt by the behavior, but it functions in keeping the prejudice alive, and therefore it must be discontinued for the prejudice to disappear. The religious Jewish man who in his daily prayers mutters, "Thank you, God, that you did not make me a woman," is by such actions, reconfirming his view of women as inferior. He would have to give up such practices to get rid of the outlook. Private actions of this sort similarly reinforce the sense of disgrace over being homosexual harbored by great numbers of men and women.

Suppose the boy already mentioned, who ridiculed the homosexual man, afterwards discovered that he himself had homosexual urges. By now, let us say, he is an adult, lives in a small town, and for much of his lifetime has felt a chronic sense of doom because of his homosexuality. True, the attitude has persisted. But everywhere in his life he is engaging in actions, small decisions, which have as their premise the belief that he is truly less worthy than others because he is homosexual. He refuses to make the acquaintance of homosexuals who live in his part of town; he takes pains to avoid them, lest he be revealed by his reactions to them. On the off chance that his boss knows he is homosexual, he elects repeatedly not to go in to demand a raise, which he himself believes he would deserve if he were heterosexual. He often initiates conversations which he thinks are heterosexual in nature. In the barbershop he chats spuriously about sports—a topic of no interest to him at all.

His sense of guilt has been with him since he made the discovery, perhaps in his early teens. If asked, he would describe his homosexuality as a damning blow, and it might never occur to him that his guilt could still be erased and his life improved. And here is where the principle I mentioned comes in. There would be no way for him to talk himself out of the belief that his homosexuality makes him inferior. His only way to rid himself of the belief would be to look back and identify the numerous moments in his life when he allowed his self-degrading opinions to motivate him, even to covert actions. If his decision not to go in for the raise is a prejudicial act, he must not engage in it no matter how he feels. On the premise that his being homosexual ought not to disqualify him, he must go for the raise. What the boss does is another matter entirely. He must not ally himself, by his action, with the view that he is undeserving.

If so simple an act as talking about sports to the barber is dishonest for him, he must desist from such pretenses. The premise of the act is that he is not really a "regular guy" as he should be. "Regular guy" means heterosexual in his view, and this is the very attitude he must be careful not to sustain. If, in fact, life would be unbearable in his town unless he kept up a detailed pretense, then his only choice is to leave. The one piece of advice given invariably by homosexual men and women across the country who are the leaders of the new movement for gay rights is for conflicted homosexuals in small towns to get out if necessary, to go to the big cities, where there are thousands of homosexuals living happily and without guilt. No matter how long demoralization has lasted, it is fair to say it would not continue if the homosexual person detected its role as a motivation for decisions and desisted from all actions based on the view of himself as inferior. It is well known that attitudes underlie actions and give rise to them. But it is also true that no attitude can survive without being expressed in action. The best way by a mile to get rid of an attitude, like chronic guilt over being homosexual, is to identify all behavior springing from the attitude and discontinue it. Changing the behavior is not merely removing a symptom, as

Freud and others have thought. It is the one sure way to change the attitude underlying it.

In other cases, the person knows he is homosexual before adopting his adult attitude toward himself for being homosexual. After a period of homosexual activity without much reflection, he crystallizes an attitude. Whether this attitude becomes guilt or pride is, in this case too, well within the power of the individual to determine.

Where a crisis occurs within the person, by choosing to act in accordance with one of several attitudes that may come to him in rapid alternation—whether it is guilt or the belief that he has the same rights as previously—he deepens his sense of its rightness. In effect, he is sowing the seeds of this attitude, whichever it is, and as it springs up, it enters as a relevant motive for a widening range of decisions to be made. The new style of life the person is creating serves to bulwark this newly elevated attitude, and as time goes by it comes to seem utterly natural. This occurs where the attitude is the sense of absolute entitlement to a good life, just as it did with guilt.

To produce this sense of entitlement to happiness, one must seize the belief that one deserves full rights and use it as a motivation for decisions wherever possible. At first the belief may come only in moments, as an emotionless thought, an occasional whisper to oneself that one deserves fair play. But this is enough. So long as it exists in some strength on some occasions, there is the chance to nourish it by decisions based on it. By being sure to act in accordance with the belief when it is felt, one raises it to a new status, elevates it into a conviction. Where the belief that one deserves utterly fair treatment becomes a dominant motive in life, it comes to seem utterly reasonable, no matter how the person felt about himself previously. The critical issue is that one must act everywhere in accordance with the premise that homosexuality should in no way be considered a detraction.

A wide variety of decisions have bearing on the homosexual's attitude toward himself. Even in seemingly insignificant ones, there is the danger that guilt, or the thought that one does not deserve perfect equality, will surreptitiously enter as a motivation.

The most relevant decisions fall into three categories.

First, there are decisions made in direct connection with the homosexual's attitude toward himself. Whether to try to change. Whether to lament being homosexual. Whether to atone by such devices as undue generosity toward people, or by lowering one's aspirations. Whether to become obsessed over searching for the "root reasons." If it is a man, whether to affect effeminate airs and graces as a justification; or, contrarily, for a woman, to affect mannishness as a justification (instead of doing so, if one wants, simply because the role is pleasurable). Whether to pursue homosexual love with full commitment.

Secondly, there are decisions made regarding other individuals in one's life. Whether to tell them. In particular, whether to tell parents, and for what reason. Whether to apologize for being homosexual. Whether to risk being seen in homosexual places. Whether to lie about a relationship with a lover. To whom. Whether to disparage heterosexual customs to justify one's own choice to be homosexual. Whether to object when others ridicule homosexuals, at the risk of being detected.

Finally, there are decisions made toward homosexuals as a group. Whether to ridicule homosexuals. Whether to disparage other people called deviates by society. Whether to avoid homosexuals who are outspoken, who are gay and proud, or to join them. Whether to join the gay liberation movement.

In making such choices, the motives for them give them their meaning. In some cases a lie may be a rational decision and not a self-derogating one at all. If one lies to a mother because she has already had four heart attacks and would be terrified by the fact of a son or daughter being homosexual, the motive for the act may be kindness. Telling the same lie, however, is self-damaging if contempt for the self is the actual motive. It would add to one's sense of shame. Indeed, the lie will push the person toward despair. It will not help if the person invents the rationalization that his motive for concealment is kindness and nothing more. Our behavior affects us in accordance with our *actual* motivations for it.

The healthy homosexual is usually someone who has discovered that the heterosexual ideal he has believed in since childhood is inapplicable in his own life. At first he felt alone, as if something gigantic were lost. But this is only an early reaction. The decision to plunge forward, to become his own boss, soon brings exhilaration. The sense that he can now do what he wants courses through the bloodstream, and he is surprised to note the recovery of an enthusiasm which had been dulled by a multitude of unidentified compromises made in the past. The person may even come to see himself as part of a great new throng—of those living in the past and present who also discovered that the ruling fictions of their day did not hold for them. In this way the person enters the domain of the true individual. He or she becomes the spiritual ally of everyone—homosexual and heterosexual—who has staked out his own path in life.

All persons who have reconsidered convention and found it wanting are able to draw nearer to one another than before. This is so, because conventionality is no longer enticing us to suppress our spirits. Conventionality can no longer sunder us by forcing us to pretend we are identical when we are not. Like Coriolanus, we have been banished from Rome and have departed proudly, saying "Rome, I banish you."

The Effortless Acceptance of Homosexuality

Some homosexuals have never seen their homosexuality as a problem.

One day last year, I asked my friend Lilli Vincenz, long a campaigner for homosexuals' rights, whether she had ever felt guilty about being homosexual. She answered thoughtfully, No, she had not. "What about you, Marcelle?" I asked her lover. "No," she said.

When I asked why not, Lilli answered, "I have always associated my ability to love with the best things in me. It was a positive feeling and not a negative one. I thought it was the best I could offer, when I loved somebody and wanted us to be happy. I always associated it with the beautiful and the true and the best I could think of, and therefore there was no shame."

"I guess I see it as working with another person toward the same ideal," said Marcelle.

I have since canvassed a number of homosexuals met outside my practice on the question of whether they had suffered guilt, and how they dealt with it. It seemed to me that a sample made up largely of persons who were emotionally troubled and had come for help might not yield a fair cross-section of answers. And as might be expected, among gay liberation leaders I found a higher percentage who had never suffered guilt.

"Why never any guilt in your case?" I asked Randolfe Wicker, one of the first in the movement to declare himself homosexual on national television. His appearance on "The Les Crane Show" in 1964 drew hundreds of letters to the societies working for homosexuals. His answer was funny, yet revealing. "Well, my mother was hard of hearing, and she was not a trusting person. So I guess people's opinions didn't matter much."

My inquiries suggest that more women than men proportionately have been able to recognize that they were homosexual without feeling disgrace. Beyond the fact that homosexuality is considered more detrimental to men, there is a reason for this. As mentioned earlier, women are more apt to make the discovery in adulthood, and frequently a woman makes it when already in love with another woman. When this happens, she is in many cases so buoyed by the relationship that the concept of herself as homosexual may seem empty and unimportant. Only when the relationship ends, if it does, may she feel guilty in some degree. At this time she may have to face being a lesbian with all the misgivings she has internalized.

The acknowledgment that one is homosexual seems to be more incumbent on men than women. In a great many cases women live together as lovers without even acknowledging that they are doing so. They never talk about lesbianism, and if they read about the subject they consider lesbians to be another breed, some sort of social pariah with whom they have nothing in common.

In contrast, great numbers of teenage boys recognize they are homosexual long before they have even met another homosexual. Before the recent wave of publicity on homosexuality, millions of teenagers were discovering to their horror that they were homosexual, and had nowhere to look for precedent. Many lived for years with the sense that they were emotionally misshapen and doomed. One man told me that he waited for five years before meeting another homosexual in his small town, that he wrote regularly in his diary, "Dear God, please introduce me to another, to just one other homosexual person, like me."

It is this kind of suffering that the courageous homosexual of today will eliminate from tomorrow.

The so-called deviant has two major possibilities to consider. He makes a grand investment whichever way he elects to play his life. He can reinvest perennially in the belief that his "deviancy"—here, his homosexuality—is a moral vice and ought to be destroyed. If so, over the years he will convince himself, more strongly than ever, that society did well to lay down its present ethic governing people like him. On the other hand, he can refuse to apologize or pay compensation in any way for being different from the majority stereotype. In this way, he is investing in himself and in a new society, whose members have lifestyles more various than those in the present one.

FIVE

COMMUNICATION WITH PARENTS

It is not surprising that difficulties with parents are among the most significant problems in the lives of many homosexuals. Psychologists, psychiatrists and writers have spread misinformation about homosexuality far and wide, and have poisoned millions of parents against young adults who have embarked on homosexual lives. The self-styled experts have been dismaying the parents of homosexuals by a number of unsubstantiated charges. An old favorite is that when a person becomes homosexual, this means his parents are at fault and also sick themselves: "A child's homosexual tendencies are a symptom of parental disturbance," wrote Dr. Toby Bieber (as quoted by Wyden).

Next, homosexuality is likened to criminal behavior in its being called the result of a botch-job by parents:

No parent sets out deliberately to produce a delinquent or a homosexual. Yet it is recognized today that delinquency and homosexuality are both rooted in the home. (Wyden)

The evidence collected over the past twenty years strongly contradicts the assertion about homosexuality. And however one feels about that evidence, an analogy can prove nothing. This one, in restating the case that parents are at fault, smuggles across to parents the notion that their homosexual sons and daughters are criminal types. This last accusation has thrown many parents hopelessly off course. Were it not for the mental health experts, millions of parents would be making independent decisions about their children's homosexuality, and many would decide that our national customs and laws here are unduly punitive. In other words, the mental health experts have cut down sharply the number of parents who rally to the side of their homosexual children.

Even the distress frequently felt in the presence of homosexual persons is made to seem natural. The Wydens talk about parents withdrawing from their children as if it were easily understandable. After calling homosexuality a sickness, they write:

Almost everybody gets anxious in the presence of abnormality. Few of us are comfortable with a deformed person. Almost everybody is happy to leave the hospital after visiting a sick friend.

But in many societies the sight of a homosexual does not cause the same repercussions. Parents are not constructed by nature to shun homosexual children. This is a decision many parents make on their own, after reading only one brand of literature on the subject. Theories change drastically on which parental behavior is supposed to produce homosexuality. But those who announce that homosexuality is an illness, and a mark of bad character, nearly always hold parents responsible, at least in part. Thus the glibness of supposed authorities has added greatly to the agony suffered by millions of parents whose children enter homosexual lives, even for a time. Not always shame, but sometimes the desire to spare their parents profound unhappiness, is behind the decision by homosexuals to leave home and wind a cocoon of secrecy around their lives.

The self-styled experts warn that the best time to catch incipient homosexuality is when children are between the ages of three and ten. But what are parents to do? For a time it was believed that a dominant mother was the cause. But when many children are born to the same parents, they show roughly the same distribution of homosexuals among them as the population at large. Why, if the parents are causal, do some children "contract" homosexuality and others not? It is possible that the parents have almost nothing to do with the matter, or nothing to do with it, in most or all cases. Perhaps, in many instances, pleasurable experiences, homosexual in nature, occurring when the mental processes are somehow impressionable and receptive, motivate the desire for more of the same. If so, in such cases, the intricate web of coincidences can take so many forms that parents are only one of a thousand factors. It might even turn out that parents who encouraged love and sensual exploration and enjoyment of life, being the ones most apt to rear children who are bright and eager, are the most likely to rear homosexual and bisexual children, as well as healthy heterosexual children. It may well be that in many cases, the more inhibited the child, the more conventional and fearful he becomes, the less likely he is to awaken sexually, and so it becomes easy for him to choose his marriage partner by conventional standards. The parent who encourages the child to use his own reactions in deciding what he likes, is a parent ready to risk his child's becoming homosexual, for the sake of the resonance of the child's whole later life.

Many theoreticians hate to backtrack. They add intricacies and twists to their theories, when data has been obtained which calls for withdrawing their theory entirely. Over a period of years, a man may put forth five different theories on how homosexuality develops in the home, and though each is different from the others, he goes on being considered an authority so long as he puts forth any one of them.

The theory that a dominant and "close-binding" mother raises homosexual sons appeared contradicted by a curious observation. Jewish mothers are proverbially dominant and "close-binding." One would expect more homosexuality among Jews than in most groups, if the theory were right. But a slightly *lower* incidence of homosexuality is found among Jews than in the country at large. Dr. Lief Braaken of Cornell supplied the reconciliation to preserve the theory in this case: "Maybe the fathers in Jewish families tend to be less detached in relation to their sons, as compared with fathers in gentile families." A quick dismissal of seemingly contradictory evidence—a dismissal accomplished by a technique too frequent in psychology, that of inventing some new twist, and though it is not proven, using it as an explanation. If the Jews had statistically proven to produce a higher fraction of homosexual sons, rather than a lower one, the new thought about the Jewish fathers would not have been invented. The finding would have been taken as confirmation of the belief that a dominant mother is a key factor for producing homosexuals.

The observation that homosexuals are raised by parents showing every conceivable pattern of traits is well documented. But it is as if the experts were determined not to let this observation deter them from holding parents accountable. To his dominant-mother theory, Dr. Irving Bieber has added an alternative:

> The child who becomes homosexual is usually overprotected and preferred by his mother. In other cases he may be underprotected and rejected. (quoted in Wyden)

Nearly any parent whose child becomes homosexual can look back and imagine he has erred in one of these two directions. These days, most of those who say parental treatment is a factor, add that many other factors operate too. As a result of propaganda from many sides, millions of parents, on discovering that their children are homosexual, sink under the weight of awful reactions. Believing that they have wrecked the life of their child and loved one, they feel demoralized and ashamed; they become furious toward the child who appears to them defiant in his delinquency. Worst of all, the child suddenly appears like a member of another species, someone whose essential wants are unrecognizable and different, and this fills many parents with inexpressible sadness.

The death blow to these relationships is usually dealt by the children themselves. No effort is made to educate the parent about homosexuality, or to convince the parent that all is not lost and that a friendship is still possible. If one lives at home and is dependent financially, the cost of confrontation is heavy. But ultimately it is wrong to take bestowals where this limits freedom, and one must depart and live independently as soon as possible. Then the decision about how much of one's life to disclose, and how to proceed, may become decisive for the relationship.

The decision may be easy if a parent has displayed indifference over the years. One may feel no need to account to such a person; for example, the father who ran off during one's childhood and who never inquired after the family or helped subsidize it. One's concern over the opinion of such a parent may be low, in comparison with the worry when one knows a parent to be dedicated but full of misinformation on the topic of homosexuality. Telling such a parent seems hazardous, unwise. But on the other hand, it seems a shame to decide alone that the parent would not have been heroic. Till now, parent and child may have confided in each other and been as one in rooting for each other's happiness. They were confidants especially when events touched them dearly. In such a relationship, it seems a shame to break the bond, on the untested premise that the parent would have broken it.

The decision that friendship with parents would be irrecoverable if the disclosure were made has been used by millions of homosexuals as an excuse for withdrawing from their parents, when the real reason was that they were ashamed of being homosexual, and felt too weak to withstand even a single word of rebuke. It seems to me, a few unhappy interludes should not be prohibitive if the possible reward is continuation of a love relationship, and this would certainly apply to relationships with parents where love is felt.

I have talked to many parents bewildered by the seemingly permanent indifference expressed toward them by children who were obviously living homosexual lives. The evidence was plain to the parents, but they had not been able to digest it. On some occasions, when parents have come to my office to discuss a son or daughter living in some other city, after weeping they have told me they would give anything for a phone call once a month, and to see their children on occasion. I usually believe them. When the child has virtually told them he was homosexual but they have resisted interpreting the hints, I have sometimes asked, "Do you think the reason could be that your son, or daughter, is homosexual and is afraid of your knowing?"

Sometimes this uproots a story of how a father punched his son or told him to leave the home. The parents knew. But allegiance to their child seemed to demand that they not betray the child's homosexuality, even to me. My discussion then centers on whether it would be worth it to them to help bring the topic out into the open, and then to say to the child that they love him. Next, if the parents are still receptive, comes the rehash of the reasons for their distress. I always advise the parents not to present the matter for a time, while they clarify their own attitudes toward homosexuality. Having a clear point of view for them is a requisite before talking to their child about his homosexuality. If they indicate that they would prefer never to discuss it, this is acceptable too. Our work together may be over. Our only result has been to bring into the open the reason why they are not intimate with their child any longer.

Parents are often astounded to learn that there are millions like them in this country—adults at all social levels—whose unspoken lifetime pact with their children has been broken by both parties, as silently as it was made many years earlier. I usually add to parents that the underlying issue has nothing to do with homosexuality; it has to do with allegiance. Anyone's child—heterosexual or homosexual—is likely to cherish the thought that in an emergency the parent would rush to his defense. When could loyalty be more opportune than now—from the point of view of the young homosexual man or woman who finds society scornful and disappointing?

Sometimes in my office I tell parents about the sixty-year-old woman who marched for her son in the first Gay Day parade in the summer of 1970. Her son was on the West Coast, when she joined the ten thousand homosexual men and women walking together up the streets of Manhattan, holding placards and singing. Included in that joyous crowd were persons of every conceivable occupation and walk of life—teachers, novelists, lawyers, dishwashers, doctors; crowds along the sidewalks; even the police were jovial—as if the city itself were telling its gay community it was sorry they had been made to suffer needlessly, and for a few hours the city would be hospitable. Nature smiled that day— perhaps because homosexuality is found everywhere in nature. Man is the only creature beneath the sun who condemns it.

The woman who marched with the gay group represented millions of mothers of homosexuals who did not come forth. In my office, I sometimes ask the parents of a homosexual if they were there. And when they say no, I ask, "Why not? What about next year? Are you too embarrassed to claim your son, the one you were once so proud of?"

But of course I cannot do this if the son or daughter has retreated and not given the parent a chance. Even the mother who drew closer to her son than ever after the Gay Day parade, would have been deprived of intimacy she apparently wanted and deserved, if her son had not believed in her.

One can't always be sure how the disclosure of one's homosexuality will be received. Sometimes the reaction is exhilarating and then one can only feel sorry that time was wasted before telling the person. In May, 1971, *The Advocate* ran a letter from a nun to a much younger brother who had told her he was homosexual after hiding the fact from her for many years:

Dear Michael,
Today you revealed to me an intimate part of your life. Something I have long suspected, but now it has been verbalized.
   I did cry for one moment; one short, yet eternal moment. I cried because you doubted my acceptance of you. I will. I always will. . . ."

The Crisis for Parents

Among heterosexuals who marry, settle down and raise children, many would have chosen the same life, even if prevailing modes were different and their behavior caused them to be outcasts. The desire to be conventional has not been their commanding motive. Their erotic fantasies have been heterosexual, predominantly or completely, and their personal philosophy has been dictating their style of life. Their lives have been rewarding for these reasons. Their children may call them conventional because of the way they live. But they may be less conventional than their children and simply doing what they want to do.

The distinction between such adults and compulsive conformists cannot be made from a casual survey of how they spend their time. Their scheduled activities may be the same; they belong to the same clubs, vote for the same candidates, the couples go south to similar hotels in the winter. As parents, both kinds of people desire a good education, respectability and the benefits of a sound income for their sons and daughters. But there is a difference in *why* they want these things. In the one case, the achievements are valued because they earn acceptance. In the other they are valued because it is believed, with some reason, that the accomplishments will improve the person's chances of being happy later on. In the former case, if a son or daughter reports having found a more pleasurable route than conformity for the sake of respectability, the parent feels defeated. The young person could expostulate in favor of his new-found mode of living till doomsday but would not receive a hearing. In presenting evidence out of his or her own experience, the person would only cause the parent to feel distraught. In any discussion that followed, the young person might be taking for granted that one ought to tolerate risks sometimes for the sake of marvellous experiences. But the parent, not holding this philosophy, could never be swayed by any argument presupposing it. The two discrepant outlooks might never be made explicit, especially if arguments on small details pertaining to the person's life became caustic.

The parent whose daily activities might appear similar but who is not commanded by the need for social respectability would, by contrast, be accessible to reason. To such a parent it means something to hear a loved one, especially one's own son or daughter, report being contented and fulfilled. Where this is said, such a parent would question his own right to give advice insistently—even if engaging in the other person's practices would be very distasteful to him. Of course, anyone has the right to remark to someone once or twice how that person's behavior might be harming him. But a suggestion is one thing, and a barrage of criticism produced by hysteria is another.

The distinction between the guiding motivations becomes evident when a grown-up son or daughter announces the discovery of happiness in a life that is unconventional. Anyone with sense knows that the way to show love is to express it when someone needs it, and may feel alone. Where the issue is homosexuality, the instinct to move toward, or away from, a homosexual son or daughter, bespeaks the dominant motive in the parent. Of course, I have been contrasting extremes for the sake of exposition. Most people are responding to some combination of motives.

Granted, a parent who believes his child is sick will understandably beseech the child to try to convert. A devoted parent who does not realize that in spite of the laws many homosexuals are happy will be dispirited by the discovery that a darling is homosexual. The parent may, out of love, feel frightened at what he or she may think is inevitable for the child—a life of persecution and loneliness. But a dedicated parent will keep faith with his child by investigating further, searching through the various points of view, learning what he can about how homosexuals live. Not all information is contained in medical books under "deviancy." Since the nineteen-fifties homophile groups have been gathering material for free distribution, and in some cities these groups have set up small lending libraries for the interested public.

It should be significant to parents that there has even been opposition to the circulation of this material. For instance, back in 1964, a congressman from Texas, who testified he thought there were no homosexuals where he came from, tried to get a bill passed which would deny homophile groups the right to solicit funds desperately needed to present their viewpoints. Congressman Dowdy did not win his case. Since 1964, in spite of stiff opposition, gay groups have proliferated. The parent who cares will talk to at least one or two representatives of these groups, and perhaps attend meetings and read some of the recommended literature.

Parents of homosexuals should consider that till recently the many who believed that homosexuality need not be a barrier to happiness have been denied the chance to marshal their case. Even now, many newspapers will not review books with this point of view, and many more will not praise them no matter how cogent they are. It is still considered by many a freak-show when homosexuals are allowed on a major network to present their case. They are usually asked in advance not to "get political," which means not to discuss the unfair penalties against homosexuals. And in many cases only homosexual men are allowed to appear. In a recent show, lesbians were prohibited even from asking questions of the panel members. When I protested this, the producer told me, "The country isn't ready for the women yet. That will be another show, sometime."

When a child's being homosexual becomes a crisis for a parent, it is usually a crisis in deciding whether to give precedence to love or conventionality as motives. Does the parent simply want the child to accomplish in society what the parent failed to do? If so, the son or daughter is a pawn for achievement, an embellishment. Or does the parent want the child to find happiness primarily? I don't say that a parent's first reaction upon learning a son or daughter is homosexual informs us of much. But the ultimate attitude of the parent tells us the parent's dominant motive: love or conventionality.

Certain problems in the home are more common among lesbians than among homosexual men. For instance, a woman is more apt to find herself being importuned by parents to marry. Women are imagined to need more guidance from mother and father until they marry; in contrast, men are often considered self-sufficient as soon as they "go out on their own." It is expected that women will welcome assistance where it is offered, and object to advice less than men do. This means that in the home daughters are subjected to the rat-tat-tat of prying questions more than their brothers are. Women are expected to enjoy confidential chats with mother. And even if they have gone far away to live on their own, there is more expectation than with young men that they will want to spend their holidays at home, at least till they are married. It is not unusual for a gay woman to be driven hundreds of miles to her hometown by a lover, there to be deposited at the local train station, while her lover drives on to her own home elsewhere—both seeking to avoid a breach with parents who expect their daughter to spend Thanksgiving or Christmas with them, more than they would a son. It is an adage in one group of gay women I know that the one sure thing lesbian couples are asked to surrender is their holidays together.

Wherever sexism operates in the home, it complicates the lesbian's task of coexistence with parents. Not just defiance but even secrecy is considered more acceptable in men than women. Consequently, it is easier for boys than girls to prevent inquiries by parents into their private lives. A homosexual young man may be able to end a father's questioning about his personal life by a wink—one timed to suggest that he is having a series of amorous adventures with lovelies better undiscussed for reasons of gallantry. The wink implies: "Take my word for it pop. I'm sowing my wild oats." When subjected to interrogation, a lesbian can hardly use the same device. And even if she announces frankly that she is happy and that marriage is not on her agenda, it is apt to be assumed that she is pretending satisfaction and is inwardly discontented. As for the disclosure to parents that one is a lesbian, lesbianism is even less familiar to the average person than homosexuality in men; and so in the case of the lesbian there would be more stupefaction to overcome, more to explain, if the truth were told.

It is interesting to observe how many homosexuals, including many who are outspoken elsewhere, avoid discussing the topic with their parents. Recently, on a TV talk show, a leader of the gay movement was asked how his parents felt about his being homosexual. He faltered that he hadn't told them, saw no point to it. "That's the one area that comes hardest to us," he admitted to the host.

At least a few representatives of the gay movement have taped talk shows, and then in the two-week interlude before they were played, have visited home for an overdue chat with mother, so that the neighborhood wouldn't surprise her with the news.

Many in the movement agree that a coming step, necessary for the sense of wholeness of the individual members, will be the encouragement of homosexuals to stop hiding the fact from their parents. Not that everyone must do this—each person decides on the merits of his own case. But the thought is that in a great number of instances the excuses for a lifetime of secrecy are invalid, and homosexuals have for too long been accomplices in the silence surrounding themselves.

Because few people broach the subject, the occasional individuals who disclose their homosexuality to parents are at a disadvantage. Such a person is apt to appear more like a solitary case than one of a giant minority, unidentified, with members scattered everywhere in the world. Any plea seems less strange if it is made by millions. If parents could quickly recall many cases in which friends of theirs had heard similar disclosures made by children, the jolt would be less. And with many models available of how other parents handled the same disclosure in the past, parents might set themselves to considering options rather than fly off the handle. The simple experience of chatting with a friend whose son or daughter made the same disclosure would be relieving. Many parents would learn that the range of possible reactions to the disclosure of homosexuality includes equanimity and continued friendship.

A comparison with the situation sometimes faced by heterosexuals who marry partners objectionable to their parents is informative. The emotionality, and even the violence, aroused in some parents, is seen often. And so is the resilience of many of these same parents. Unlike the homosexual, who decides whether to discuss his life with his parents, and can avoid doing so, the heterosexual who marries "the wrong partner" is out in the open. In the great majority of cases, on seeing that their route of access to their child demands that they stop complaining about the marriage, they grow to accept it. If homosexuals would make their case clearly, that the parents' love is still wanted if offered respectfully, more relationships would be preserved. Here, as with the father who makes physical threats to the suitor of a favorite daughter, parents in great numbers would prove themselves flexible and loyal later on.

The decision to conceal one's homosexuality, when made, is usually based on the judgment that one's parents would react inhumanely, would never understand. This makes the choice a prejudgment. Who can be sure that the parents, after storming, would not have come round and stuck by their own children? The breaking of what was once a bond of communication of precious importance, on the premise that the parents would have broken it, is a decision to water down the relationship. It represents surrender of the chance for the frankest possible communion with the parents. In some cases, it means giving up this possibility for intimacy on the mere hunch that the parent would prove unworthy of it.

Besides, it means disowning the truth. And telling the truth is an excellent device for coping with interrogations: "I don't date girls, mother. You forget. As I told you last month, I do not plan to get married, as things now stand. Of course, anything can happen, theoretically. But as I see it, I am homosexual and if possible will go on living with Tom, my lover, the man you don't want to meet."

Sometimes the decision not to tell parents is based on the belief that they would be *right* to feel revolted. In such a case, there is special reason to tell them. Divulgence can reduce inner turmoil, especially if the job is done well—even if a parent becomes distraught and wildly unreasonable. By telling, the person is acting boldly on the premise that his being homosexual should not disqualify him from enjoying the full backing of people who care about him, in this case his parents. Even if his parents oppose him, he has externalized the struggle. With them as adversaries, he becomes free to act purely as an advocate of his own rights.

Even in the midst of heated arguments, this thought brings exhilaration.

When a person decides not to trust in parents, and the chief motivation is his own misgivings about being homosexual, the secrecy tends to reinforce the misgivings. If you conceal any trait because it embarrasses you, you will increase your sense of shame over it. After a time, you may make it seem reprehensible. Many homosexuals who kept dread silence during the past decades have thoroughly convinced themselves that a disclosure even now would be disastrous. Some are appalled at the openness in the new group of gay liberationists. To the older generation, telling parents seems out of the question. But the new generation does not have this history. Telling parents is getting easier. Where there has been a frank and intimate relationship between parent and child, the decision to gamble on the parent's continued loyalty has much to be said for it.

On the other hand, sometimes there are destructive motives for making the disclosure; such motives are well worth searching for, and nullifying if they are present. One of these is the desire to be punished—call it *moral masochism* if you wish; the other is *hostile defiance*. With the first, one hopes that the parents will disapprove, be shocked, even recommend therapy for cure—do anything but countenance the homosexuality. With defiance, the man or woman wants there to be a violent confrontation with the parents.

Where moral masochism is operating, one wants to make the parents appear as decent as possible. The disclosure is made like a religious confession, and the parent punishes or forgives. By assigning the role of high priest to one's mother or father, the homosexual creates possibilities for relief from his own guilt. He can suffer now, if his parents excoriate him, instead of having to anticipate suffering later. Forcing the moment to its crisis in this way is a frequent motive for confessionals. Also, by attributing the special power of judgment to the parents, though one becomes liable to castigation, there is the possibility that if the parents relent, one can bask in forgiveness. Like others suffering from persistent guilt, the homosexual sometimes tries to relieve it by disclosing his homosexuality to the most "decent" people he can find, in the hope that even if they are shocked at first, they will grant him, or her, at least an inkling of acceptance later on. To the acutely guilty person, the value of this may seem well worth the confession.

Like masochism, the defiance motive is usually activated by guilt. Here too the parent is elevated to a position of undue importance. But the aim this time is not to have someone on hand for the expiation of one's sins. This time one wants a minister, full-fledged and in flowing robes, in order to shred those robes, to make the person look ignorant, incompetent, preposterous—and thus to debunk society's position by discrediting an individual. Efforts are made to prod the parents into making foolish statements, into betraying dogmatism to the degree that they appear as caricatures.

The idea that by discrediting an individual, one can depreciate the seeming importance of the attitude thought to be embodied in the person, is in error. The opposite effect is more likely. Persistent assaults on persons considered to embody particular opinions renew one's preoccupation with the people and their opinions.

Social masochism and defiance as motives for the disclosure that one is homosexual both bode continued difficulty with parents. With both there is provocation causing unnecessary suffering. Sensing that he or she is harassing the parents, the young homosexual is likely to feel guilty for new reasons. And the delegation of undue power to anyone is harmful in the long run, since it amounts to the surrender of some degree of personal freedom.

When giving vent to hostile motives, the homosexual is using his or her parents like hired actors asked to play special parts so that the person can clarify his own position—and justify it. The parents are thought of as agents for a particular point of view, and the aim of the game is to get them to perform in particular ways. When more genuine motives operate, the ultimate intention is to build a bridge to the parent. The stakes are higher.

The person about to tell a parent has much to consider. I want to list some of the issues now, and to make some suggestions. But it should be remembered that no suggestion can be universally applicable.

1. Often it is a good idea to discuss homosexuality generally, to allow them to talk on the topic, before disclosing that one is homosexual. Much information can be imparted this way, and if one becomes suspect in the process, this can make the disclosure easier. If the mere mention of the topic makes the parent incoherent, this may be a sign to postpone discussing one's case. Sometimes, the allusion to the topic has touched

suspicions still unconscious in the parent—the hysterical reaction is to the thought that one's darling may be a homosexual. The parent is asking in advance, "Say it isn't so." Still, it may be possible and worthwhile to introduce information on homosexuality slowly, and eventually to present the truth about oneself.

2. Remember that the right to say you are homosexual to anyone at any time is precious. Never agree not to tell this—say to a father, if mother makes the request. You may want to keep it a secret from him, or you may not. Some confidants will want to use the special knowledge as a way of drawing a son or daughter closer, even as a way to win the child from the other parent. Mother may whisper, "Don't ever tell your father." But the answer cannot be Yes. There is no need to close a door to anyone. Your response to your own homosexuality is far too personal to be decided by anyone else.

3. Avoid blame. Blame is an implicit assertion by you that homosexuality is bad. Or its purpose is sheerly to inflict pain. As an example: "You messed me up, mother. If you hadn't gone to work and been so ballsy, I would not be the freak that I am!"

This sort of presentation is not so unusual as one might think; it is an act of sadism, and perhaps of masochism too. The intent is to cause suffering, and if one loves the parent, sometimes it is also to suffer as the parent weeps. The presentation has no hope of building a bridge to the parent.

Similarly, avoid subtler forms of blame. I mean quiet references to "how it happened," or to failings in the parent; these feed the other person's sense of guilt. The need to inflict pain suggests that the presentation is premature. The resolved homosexual who discusses his life openly with one or both parents considers the matter of blame to be pointless, ignorant and insulting. And since he or she does not want the parent to suffer more than necessary, the person is prompt to object if the parents introduce the concept of blame and berate themselves. "Mother, there is no need to reconsider your handling of me when I was a child. I am not a tragedy. You did an excellent job."

4. Avoid apologies: "I'm sorry I won't be marrying the boy next door and having children." A woman said this to her aging father. The apology was insincere. It was an act of defiance—as if she were saying, "I know you are a highly conventional person and would never understand. . . ."

Apologies are not in order unless one has committed a harmful or irresponsible act. No sexual act entered into voluntarily by adults calls for apology. When not hypocritical, apologies for such acts are pathetic.

5. Watch your tone of presentation. It will linger in the listener's memory and will influence the person's reaction to what is being said. The parent will very likely be making judgments on the spot regarding how your being homosexual is influencing you. This means that sudden, hostile defensiveness, or a blunt manner when asked simple questions, can undo the possible value of an otherwise reasonable presentation.

6. Be emotionally prepared for an explosive reaction. The test is not how parents respond the first minute after being told. It is how they respond after they have had some time to think the matter over. Remember that they have very likely been influenced by what they have read on the subject.

7. Don't answer insincere or rhetorical questions.

8. Be ready to familiarize your parents with what it means to be a homosexual. At the very least, if they are willing, they might profit by being given literature on the subject. If possible, they should get to meet gay people who are productive and are enjoying their lives. Such people abound in homophile groups and elsewhere these days.

9. Be ready to end the discussion quickly if it gets out of hand. Outbursts are usually a sign not to go on. As dangerous are the innuendos that may enter what began as a well-behaved dialogue. Where it is recognized that nothing more can be accomplished in a given session, the discussion should be ended gracefully if possible. If the parent has shown signs of reasonableness, or at least of the desire to expend effort to understand the young adult, a compliment may well be in order. In any event, the flexibility to stop on a dime is important. The possible accomplishments of good discussion can sometimes be sullied in a matter of minutes. One can do only so much in a single session. One can always wait till another day.

10. It is often worth making explicit the good will behind the disclosure. "Dad, you know I didn't have to tell you. I wanted you to know because I love you and wanted you to understand me." Sometimes parents can see that in telling, a youngster had nothing to gain except intimacy, and much to lose by way of being discredited and abandoned. This fact may be worth pointing out as part of a request for an honest hearing.

11. Consider that if a parent ridicules a lover, he is ridiculing you. This fact must be pointed out, whether other action is taken or not. If the parent avers he is

certain of his reproaches, one possibility is to tell the parent to make them directly to the person being discussed. It would be fairer for the parent to pick up a phone and present his case to the lover than to berate the lover continuously to you. That way the debate will stay between the parent and the person supposedly loathesome to the parent.

I often favor this plan because the lover, being an outsider with respect to the parents, will usually suffer less than the son or daughter. So long as we cherish intimacy with our parents, they remain among the least dispensable people in our lives. This means we feel handcuffed fighting for an issue, if we are not already fully resolved on the issue. To "the outsider," the parent is simply one more meddlesome person—to be handled tactfully if possible. This gives the other person more room to protect himself, or herself, or withdraw completely if necessary. I don't believe that anyone should be forced to sit patiently while someone dear to that person is being disparaged. A parent's attack on a lover is entirely a matter for the two of them to thrash out. If the parent is too cowardly to call the lover, this should not be your problem. If the lover "can't take it," or as is more frequent, you don't have enough faith in the liaison to risk the lover's being insulted once or twice, this fact should be duly noted in your own mind.

12. What if the parents set out maliciously to ruin your life? There are such folks in existence. I personally met a handful of homosexual men and women whose parents retaliated against them for their homosexuality by going to their bosses, their teachers, their friends, and asking each to do his worst. I met a young woman

in Washington, D.C., whose parents went to the medical school where she was a student and had her
thrown out. I have heard of two cases in which fathers
went to high authorities in the armed forces about their
sons, who were then dropped dishonorably, one after
being imprisoned for a year. And several times I have
successfully begged for mercy when parents had made
threats of the magnitude mentioned.

Vindictiveness, in this measure, is rare. But the
threat of violence is an act of violence. In my opinion,
after asking the parent whether he or she still means
the threat, if the answer is still Yes, an act of violence has been committed. The first step must be to
renounce all favors and services from the parent; the
next must be to remove yourself from the parent as
cleanly as possible, and not to consider resuming communication unless the parent makes a convincing apology, if then. If one is up against a bitter jungle animal,
one must know this fact and defend oneself accord-
ingly.

13. If a well-meaning parent starts listing possible
losses caused by a homosexual life, this can become a
painful harangue to listen to. I mean a barrage of questions like, "Won't you miss having children?" "Won't
people look at you in the street?"

It becomes pointless after a time to have to cope
with every objection. The faint nausea one can feel
after answering a half-dozen questions like this may
precede the realization that the questions are barely
disguised attacks. The respondent is being forced repeatedly to defend his virtues, as evidenced in his or
her choice of homosexuality. One must stop answering questions and identify what is going on. Parent:

"Won't people look at you in the street?" Answer: "Maybe. But whatever I'm up against will not be lessened by your lecturing me now. I wish you would drop the interrogation, please." The answers that homosexuals are unrecognizable as such, or that being looked at is unimportant alongside happiness, may be worth presenting sometime. But such answers prolong discussion of the subject, and the offering of any defense may increase the nausea I mentioned.

14. Rehearse the presentation—to ensure its calmness and efficiency. One can do this alone but even better by getting someone else to play the role of parent and to try out different kinds of responses.

There are some points to keep in mind if one is a parent, and a son or daughter has told you about being homosexual.

Some Tips for Parents

1. Understand that your son's or daughter's decision to discuss the matter with you is itself a major moment in the person's life. Your reaction now, your degree of decency, will be remembered by your son or daughter forever. "What did your mother say when you told her?" This question will probably be asked of your son or daughter from time to time all during his or her life. And even if it were never asked, it would come up in the person's own reflections. When people ask your son or daughter, "How did your father react?" they are asking, "Does he love you? Did he allow the popular propaganda and his own desire for community re-

spectability to separate him and you? Too bad you didn't have a different kind of parent." If he was on your side, how lucky you are to have had even one parent who said, "I'm glad you told me."

2. When anyone reveals a piece of his own life that to him or her has important personal meaning, this is an expression of deep trust. The communication is contained as much in how the person *feels* as in what he or she says. How does your grown-up son, or daughter, feel about being homosexual? About making the disclosure to you?

Show interest and the desire to learn more, without judging your son or daughter.

3. Don't give advice. Advice is virtually never sought and almost invariably given. The parent's distress at the thought of having a homosexual in the family produces mania and the parent suddenly imagines that he is an expert on homosexuality. If you as a parent can get through the whole chat without giving *any* advice, you will be exceptional. Unless you have met many homosexuals in all walks of life, and read extensively on the subject, been following the gay liberation movements, and reading the books by homophobes, you don't have a rounded picture anyhow.

4. Do not interfere with your son's or daughter's personal doings, as for instance by not reporting telephone calls when you took the message. Deprivation in this form will do nothing but hurt and antagonize the person.

5. If years ago you shut the door on a homosexual son or daughter, and are sorry, do something. Arrange to talk to the person alone—on the phone if necessary, as sometimes occurs when the person is living in a far-away city. If you have the courage, tell

the person that you don't care whether he or she is gay, if this is how you feel. Say that you love your son or daughter. At this it would take a heart of stone to rebuff you. But act before it is too late. Do not let wistfulness replace courage.

6. Finally, remember that if you ever bring pressure against a son or daughter for engaging in homosexual acts, you yourself are being unethical. Dr. Franklin Kameny, tireless crusader for the rights of homosexuals, has made this case, as perhaps your son or daughter would like to present it:

> If the disadvantages, disabilities, and penalties which the homosexual faces are a result of society's prejudices—and of course they are, in their entirety—then suggesting that the homosexual improve his lot by submission to those prejudices, at cost of his personal integrity, is fundamentally immoral. One does not propose to solve the problems of anti-Semitism by conversion of Jews to Christianity, much as that might improve the life of many individual Jews. The homosexual has a right to remain a homosexual, and in fact a moral obligation to do so, in order to resist immoral prejudice and discrimination.

SIX

WORDS FOR THE NEW CULTURE

In New York City, two dedicated and courageous young men, Jack Nichols and Lige Clarke, undertook to create a newspaper for the gay community and others, which would be unabashed in its presentation of issues crucial to homosexuals. The newspaper was given the title *Gay*. At first, many newsdealers refused to handle the paper, which bears the letters G A Y in big print on the frong page. It was a daring experiment. But Jack and Lige believed that the time and place were right for it—or almost right, and that the paper itself would make them right. They themselves were already well known in the gay community for their efforts to get public policies toward homosexuals changed. They had joined marches and had even picketed in front of the White House as homosexuals.

Having been active for homosexuals' rights for some

time, I was introduced to Jack and Lige just as they got their paper under way, and I was very appreciative of their offer to submit pieces to it. Since then I have been a frequent contributor to their paper, which due to their talent and tenacity, has enjoyed an ever increasing popularity. Like *The Advocate,* which is published in Los Angeles, *Gay* has done wonders at giving homosexuals the sense that there can be boundless happiness in life if one is willing to reach for it.

It is unfortunate that these and other publications intended for the gay community are still read by only a small minority of homosexuals. Many of the big newspapers will still not accept ads for them; and though they are not illegal, there are many newsdealers and distributors who will not handle them. When they do reach the corner newsstand, perhaps the majority of homosexuals are reluctant to buy them. Among the purchasers of these and other publications directed toward homosexuals, many prefer to buy by subscription. Both *Gay* and *The Advocate* are directed mainly toward men. But both are eager for more women as readers, and as writers.

This chapter contains some excerpts from pieces that appeared in *Gay,* with the exception of one which was published in the magazine *Sexual Behavior.*

The traditional standard for accepting new meanings of words is the "amount of usage by people considered literate." By this criterion, many words should already have earned dictionary status but have not. In this first section, I want to discuss some of the language used by the gay community.

The Etymology of the Word "Gay"

Almost certainly the word "gay" was introduced during a period when it was felt that ambiguity was needed for safe communication. After a time, some few of such words invented for secret communication pass through the stage of being hip usages into that of being good words in common parlance, and "gay" now enjoys such a status.

In effect, the word "gay" has survived and taken on a new meaning in the last ten years. Fortunately, words like "queer" and "freak," both still sometimes used even by homosexuals to mean homosexual, have not done nearly as well. This is a testimony to the selective process going on in the minds of many homosexuals who are deciding on self-referent words. Such choices are being made continually. Those that appeal to the most people will enter the language the fastest. And in the case of homosexuals, those chosen will constitute some of the data serving to shape the view of themselves which homosexuals in the future will hold.

Such choices of self-reference are part of the heritage that homosexuals will leave to one another over generations. Since all heritage of attitude is cultural and not hereditary, it makes as much sense for homosexuals to think of themselves as an ongoing continuous group as it does for royal families who are able to boast of their direct lineage over centuries.

In fact, as I see it, the strongest bond possible among human beings is identity of attitude. We are closer to those who felt like us in the past than to those who spawned our grandparents, unless by coincidence they felt as we did.

Especially in this period of developing acceptance of homosexuality, it behooves homosexuals to examine their own language. I have known people who used words like "queer," "freak" and "pervert" about themselves (some of them smiling faintly when they did), without ever realizing that they were belittling themselves and making things harder for others.

Homophile

Any humane person who has given serious attention to the status of the homosexual in our society, and pitches in to help—even by arguing the cause at cocktail parties. The practice of attributing homosexuality to all homophiles bespeaks the thought that people are not capable of sympathy for others but only of self-seeking motives. It is a practice that puts decent people in exactly the category that homophobes put them in. Most heterosexuals so fear the charge of homosexuality that even if their hearts tell them to fight for the cause of homosexuals, they are hesitant. Homosexuals must not make the mistake of discreditng people of good will who side with them.

The best definition of a homophile was given by Dr. Franklin Kameny off the cuff, when interrogated about a heterosexual member of the Washington Mattachine Society in 1964:

She is a civilized person who wants to see a discriminated-against group of people—she wants to see their status improved in precisely the same sense that there are many, many, many whites who are active members of the NAACP, and in fact officers, and I am sure there are many Christians who are members of B'nai B'rith Antidefamation League. They are civilized people who don't like to see other people persecuted and discriminated against.

Permissible Versus Preferable

To this day, the public tends to confuse two arguments connected with homosexuality. The first is the viewpoint of the homophile movement—that homosexuality between consenting adults should be *permissible,* that the participants should incur no penalties for it. Often confused with this is the notion that homosexuality is *preferable.* Though virtually no one maintains this, many imagine they are hearing it said and become horrified at the homophile movement. Also, the homophile movement is sometimes falsely accused of making the case for *preferability,* so as to discredit its case for *permissibility.*

The words "permissible" and "preferable" suggest viewpoints that are diametric opposites. The idea that there should be no proselytizing for *any* sexual orientation as preferable is the very cornerstone of the case being made by the homophile movement. Gay liberation implies freedom from having to align oneself in sexual preference with dictates from anywhere. The idea is that sex is an expression of individuality. One difficulty is that the mere mention of homosexuality conjures up visions of sex acts in many people's minds, whereas the concept that liberty is worth preserving is more abstract. And yet the abstract idea has immense practical implications for people's happiness.

Coming Out

A change of mind produced by a change in action. The action consists of exposing to others some fact about oneself previously considered shameful and withheld. The action may be a direct disclosure, as in saying on "The David Susskind Show" that one is homosexual; or it may consist merely of allowing the trait to be guessed, as when walking into a gay bar for the first time, or down the street hand-in-hand with a lover.

But "coming out" most properly refers to the *change of mind* consequent on the bold actions. For instance, the person is a homosexual, or a transvestite, or a Jew, or is light-skinned and has decided to rejoin his black friends and be recognized as one of them. The change of mind centers on a vital truth: that repercussions are never as awful as they seem when contemplated from the shadows.

An old pal of mine, Billy ——, had been ashamed of being homosexual; he was coming out slowly till an incident blasted him out, and he has been happy ever since. He was an accountant for a construction company and gave reports to six vice-presidents who would meet around a huge mahogany table. Each had his own phone there. The group was listening to Billy tell of negotiating a delay on repayment of a loan. They were very happy at his handling of the bank president, when the conference phone rang. They picked up the receivers of their phones around the table, in time for all of them to hear the gruff voice of the foreman of one of their work crews calling in from the field. "Hey I want you to hear this." He went on nonstop. "That

Billy ———, who works for you, is a homosexual. I just wanted you to know. A faggot. He sucked my cock on his trip to check up out here. Will you please tell him to leave me alone next time he comes around."

The six receivers went down almost in unison. One of the vice presidents said impatiently, "Billy, it's marvellous that you got us six months on the repayment of the first two hundred and fifty thousand dollars, but are we stuck with a demand loan on the other deal? . . ." Billy went on with his report. There was nothing else to do. Later he argued vehemently on a financial matter with another vice-president. But no one mentioned the phone call. There was too much else to talk about. As the group put their papers in their portfolios and started filing out, they congratulated him on the deal once more. He had made considerable money for all of them. One of them, who frequently engaged in heated arguments with Billy at the conference table, added, "By the way, don't give that phone call a thought." "No," added another bigwig. "He's fired." Fortunately, there was no homophobia in the particular group, who were all heterosexual, as far as Billy knew, and were married with families. Or if there was homophobia, Billy's talents had overcome it in the particular case. The nightmares of the guiltiest homosexuals sometimes assume the form of one's being found out in a dramatic way, as Billy was. Billy had previously endured such nightmares. But he told me that after the incident, he never had a nightmare on the subject of his being exposed as a homosexual, and was very relieved as a result of the episode.

Homosexuality and Creativity

So many creative artists are now known to have been homosexual that a misconception has become widespread. It is that homosexuals possess some special ability to create.

Whether one is homosexual, though, isn't the issue. The issue is how one reacts to whatever he is. Anyone worried about what will come out of his unconscious is a lousy artist. Such a person may make a good certified public accountant, but the artist needs unabashed readiness to seize and enjoy whatever he finds in himself. This includes full willingness to experience his own sexuality, the welcoming of the body and its urges into the kingdom of the mind. The guilty person dips into the well of his abilities furtively, and this is so whether one is homosexual or heterosexual. Does the person treat part of himself as a stranger? One must not close the gates against the thrust of his own sexuality or he will need to spend half of his time like a vigilant watchman being sure that the stranger is kept out. What Freud called the fear of the return of the repressed is the disease that rots creativity.

There are three chief reasons why homosexuals have sometimes been thought intrinsically gifted as artists, which they are not. The first has to do with a lucky break which homosexuals have had. (And here, I am discussing homosexual men, and not women, since the misconception concerns men.) In both of the greatest eras of creativity—during the Golden Age in Greece and during the Renaissance, especially in Italy—it was feasible for homosexual youths to partake in profoundly emotional love relationships with older men without hideous and unwarranted interference. From the youngsters' side the gifts bestowed in these relationships were youth and love and beauty and curiosity. For all this the recompense of painstaking and loving tutelage has seemed fair.

The gift of loving dedication of tutors for students has been most apt to occur where there was love, and this has meant sexual love. Hard cash forked over by a parent for private lessons in art could never purchase the detail or dedication in training which has been poured forth in a romantic relationship. Relationships of this sort were incendiary to the splendid proliferation of genius in the creative arts in both ancient Greece and in Italy. The greater the artist, the less likely it is that without love he will dedicate himself as a tutor, spreading all his learning patiently like a carpet at the feet of a youth.

Love bestows the perception of beauty where others do not see it, and love teaches this perception.

Analogous heterosexual relationships have been rarer. Over the ages, boys have been sent off to study with male teachers, and girls have been sent nowhere. And when on occasion the man has been lover to the girl aspiring to genius, he has seen his role mainly as to protect her and not to enhance her. One can bet, though, that those whom Sappho loved had, in their season of grace, a finer chance to cultivate their talents as poets than before or after that.

The second and third reasons for the misconception that homosexuality underlies artistic flair are these. Homosexuality has always been more prevalent than has been admitted. Choose *any* hundred people at random.

Send a college of scholars to trace the details of how they spent their days, and more homosexuality in the group will be uncovered than most people would anticipate. The lives of outstanding creative artists have been subjected to this sort of scholarship. The amount of homosexuality revealed in the biographies of artists seems high particularly when contrasted with the usual underestimate of the amount of homosexuality in the total population.

Finally, in our highly competitive culture, homosexual men have an advantage in being under less pressure to conform emotionally, and if they do not fear their homosexuality, are freer to acknowledge variety in their own experience. Our culture teaches men a dread of passivity, as bordering on effeminacy, which it does not. Anyone not subject to this fear is in a fine position to welcome diverse experience, to be emotionally lifted by beauty, to weep or rejoice with animation, both extremes being considered improper for the ideal American man.

Despite other, more immediate motivations, like anger, or the desire to make money, creativity is an act of love. Every work of art is a gift. The artist in every case is creating something that is missing in his life with the aim of giving it to an envisoned person, or community of others, who also feel the lack of it. Whether a homosexual person is bestowing the gift, or a heterosexual one, does not matter. What is essential is that one feels the freedom to render the gift. The content of one's sexual fantasies, or real-life choices, is not the issue. The issue is whether the person is constantly warring against insurrections of his spirit or allowing himself to surge on the crest of his passion.

Homophobia

When defining a pattern of attitudes, like homophobia, one starts out by merely identifying the condition —here, the revulsion toward homosexuals and often the desire to inflict punishment as retribution. As with a physical condition, once a psychological state has been properly labeled, those interested in learning more about it busy themselves at identifying correlates of it. What can one say about homophobes? A colleague of mine, Kenneth Smith, who read a paper of mine on homophobia, did one of the first pieces of research on homophobia that I know of. Very likely, there will be hundreds of such studies in the future (as there have been thousands of research studies on the prejudice against blacks in recent years), and so I am happy to report on this one as possibly the first of its kind.

Kenneth Smith is a highly trained researcher and a fine therapist too. His first step was to write out a set of nine items, which he called "the Homophobic scale." Ken honed the phrasing of these items closely. The answer Yes to six of these and No to three of them indicates homophobia. Here is the list, with the homophobia responses checked in:

1	Homosexuals should be locked up to protect society.	x yes	__ no
2	It would be upsetting for me to find out I was alone with a homosexual.	x yes	__ no
3	Homosexuals should be allowed to hold government positions.	__ yes	x no
4	I would not want to be a member of an organization which had any homosexuals in its membership.	x yes	__ no

| 5 I find the thought of homsexual acts disgusting. | x | |
| | yes | no |

| 6 If laws against homosexuality were eliminated, the proportion of homosexuals in the population would probably remain about the same. | | x |
| | yes | no |

| 7 A homosexual could be a good President of the United States. | | x |
| | yes | no |

| 8 I would be afraid for a child of mine to have a teacher who was homosexual. | x | |
| | yes | no |

| 9 If a homosexual sat next to me on a bus I would get nervous. | x | |
| | yes | no |

Ken sprinkled these nine items among others into a questionnaire consisting of twenty-four items in all. "The remaining fifteen items were created to sample opinions on varied issues." He then had a set of instructors give the twenty-four-item questionnaire to 130 students at his university. The students (who were told nothing of the purpose of the study) took their questionnaire forms home and filled them out in private. Ken got 93 questionnaires back (a 77% return) and determined a "homophobia score" for each of his 93 respondents. The highest possible score was 9, the lowest was zero. He then identified the group highest on homophobia and the one lowest, keeping 22 in each of these groups and putting aside the rest of the questionnaires. So far he had not considered how his subjects (who were both male and female) answered the remaining items.

Ken's sample was admittedly small. To use more high-powered statistical techniques than he chose would have been pedantry. This was merely a pilot study—a systematic canvassing and an attempt to see where conclusions could be drawn about the population he studied. For instance, his sample was too small to reveal fundamental differences in attitude between men and women, if there were any. But even in his small sample—and smallness of sample makes it *harder,* not easier, to demonstrate relationships—Ken found a remarkable number of connections which, as a group, were almost certainly not a chance phenomenon.

He found that homophobes tended to say Yes significantly more than nonhomophobes did to the following four statements:

1. "My country right or wrong" is a very admirable attitude.
2. It is only natural to find the thought of mental illness disturbing.
3. Sexual fidelity is vital to a love relationship.
4. Although I don't always like to admit it, I would like friends to see me with a big house and fine car after I graduate.

The homophobes tended to disagree significantly more than the others with the following three statements.

1. There is nothing wrong with a man's being passive when he feels like it.
2. A belief in God is not so important to the maintenance of morality.
3. The income and professional level of a job are not so important to me as being happy with the work I do.

On the remaining eight statements there was no demonstrable difference between the homophobes and the others. Ken described his research as "exploratory" and "tentative." But pilot studies like his seldom yield as high a proportion of items that discriminate as sharply. At several junctures, Ken deliberately employed methods making it harder, not easier, for the experiment to reveal trends. The use of these safeguards was deliberate. And so the findings—the so-called significant differences he obtained—were unlikely to be a consequence of experimental bias. How far we can generalize is a matter for future investigation. I believe that other experimenters giving the Kenneth Smith questionnaire to other groups will confirm what he found. And of course new items will be invented and the question answered whether they receive different responses from homophobes and others.

Studies like this are immensely valuable. The very knowledge that homophobia is being investigated—its correlates and its roots in the personality—helps people keep in mind that homophobia is a personal problem. The mere fact of such study, as it gets publicized, may give great numbers of people second thoughts about holding the attitude.

SEVEN

THE DREAD OF BEING ALONE

On the phone a man said he wanted to talk to me with his wife. He said their marriage was on the rocks and they were both worried about it. I sensed a blasé note, which I assumed might be his way of handling massive anxiety.

I told him I would want to talk to each of them alone before seeing them together. I wanted to give them each the chance to tell me things being withheld from the other, if there were any.

He introduced himself urbanely, and I escorted him into my office. He was immaculately groomed—in a custom-made suit and well-polished shoes. He told me he had been married for four years. Before that, all his sexual contacts had been with men. His wife had been told nothing about them till an argument a year ago, when he blew up at her and disclosed them.

Recently, she had become suspicious that his friend, who was collaborating with him on a play in the evenings, was also his lover. This was so, but he had persistently denied it.

I said to him, "Suppose I asked you to sign a document saying that you promise not to have sexual relations with men during the next ten years. And there was to be a heavy penalty if you broke it. Would you sign it?"

"God. Never," he yelped.

"Suppose I had made it 'women' instead of 'men'?" I asked.

"I could do that easily," he answered. In response to further questioning he said that at no time in his life had he felt otherwise. He had married because "I thought it would change."

Now he was planning to put into my hands the task of giving him zest for females in general, and for his wife in particular.

Such an assignment is more than any psychologist living or dead could have handled. However, it is no stigma on psychotherapists that we have failed. The real stigma would be on us if we had succeeded. For then we would have been stamping out one aspect of human variety, one facet of human possibility—merely because it distressed us to think about that possibility.

He mentioned several other friends, older and presumably more experienced in life, who told him that his homosexuality was rooted in fear of women. He had felt, therefore, that by marrying a woman who was genial and very attractive, and by persevering, he could make the whole experience wonderful.

More important, he had envisioned a developmental

sequence, which had included childhood, going to school, graduating, getting married, becoming a parent, making a sum of money, dying, leaving the money to his children, and finally being forgotten. After four years of unrelieved indifference to his wife, he now felt hemmed-in by her. In recent months his indifference had turned into repugnance toward her, and especially at the thought of touching her.

He had stopped having sexual intercourse with her years ago, and in the last year each had been careful not to appear nude in front of the other. But he still allowed her to believe that he might soon desire her again.

When I asked him why, he answered that it was "kind" to allow her that hope. Actually, by concealing his homosexuality, he had disposed her to believe the worst about herself, that she was in fact repulsive and that perhaps another woman might have aroused him sexually.

Her story corroborated his. She had grasped his distaste for her but did not want to acknowledge it. She was persevering, not out of love but out of the desire to avoid failure in marriage.

She too had responded to the notion that there was a developmental scale, and now she was on the rung marked "marriage." She had leaped to her perch without knowing what was there. Now she knew, and the two of them were wretched together. Even if they were to be separated for an indefinite period, as for instance, if a war had torn them apart and sent them to different countries, there is no predicting that either would have made a happier relationship with someone else.

The person who tries to plot the direction for his

life solely by learning from others how it ought to be, and who disregards the messages of his own impulses, is in deep trouble—whether that person is heterosexual or homosexual. No matter which way you turn him, he will follow the crowd. Or what he thinks is "the crowd."

Think of the difference between the two approaches to life. If you assume that we all ought to be the same, you raise the possibility that you may be a deviate—and this has an awful implication. The next step in that direction is to withdraw from pursuing aspirations, and to solidify the belief that as a deviate you *deserve* less—that it would be a mockery to ask for all you once thought possible.

But suppose that we, members of the human family, are truly unlike one another—we are unlike one another and the choices we make as individuals render us more unlike one another every day.

Under this supposition, we are all deviates—each from the rest of us.

In this sense, none of us can be more deviate than others, since *to exist is to be deviate.*

This was the truth the young man would have to live with. And there was also the truth that his efforts to hide his separateness by spurious efforts to belong, such as his marriage, could only wither him prematurely, and embitter him.

It is easy to confuse one's special condition with the deep sense of aloneness felt by every living human who reflects on his life, and about which nothing can be done. Homosexuals must not err in paying sizeable fractions of their incomes to experts in the hope of getting rid of this aloneness.

Let me tell you what I mean.

It has always seemed to me that were I born a king, it would be awfully hard to convince me that others had pains and problems like me in my high, lonely station. Similarly, were I singled out as unfit, for whatever reason, by an indignant majority, were I told their doors were forever closed to me, it would be difficult not to connect that sense of utter aloneness which each of us feels, with my being unwanted because I was different from others.

As a writer and a practicing therapist, with all the supposed advantages, let me assure you that a muffled sense of aloneness in me is never so quiet that if I listen I cannot hear its pulse. It is a sense that some promise of life was broken, I don't know when—that somewhere exists a larger group, a mainstream, a homogeneous mass of people rejoicing and loving behind closed doors, which I cannot and will never enter. It is on this sense that I wish to focus, the terrible appreciation that I am unique and apart, forever unable to touch other people as I should like, to show them that I am one of them, to embrace them with the ultimate and consummate rejoicing, which Blake has described as taking place only in Heaven.

For any member of a minority group, it is hard not to attribute this aloneness at least in part to the banishment of which one is reminded daily. One always has the dream that being socially welcomed can somehow make the difference. There is the hope of being steeped in the living existence from which one is now excluded, and this hope motivates some people to do almost anything in order to belong. One must not confuse existential aloneness (a universal experience) with aloneness produced by the quarantines of the day.

As a therapist, suffering from much of the same aloneness, I have watched homosexual patients, and others, downgrading themselves and hiding their tastes even from friends of their own choosing—all in the misguided hope of someday gaining admission into an envisioned Palace of Crystal. It is my job to convince them that *what seems like a forfeit owed for the life they chose is instead a price paid by each of us simply because we live and are conscious*. Once he realizes that his pain of separateness is universally shared, the homosexual becomes less likely to flagellate himself, less likely to imbue the culture with power to crush him. He becomes less ready to engage in self-impinging attempts to belong—and these attempts include trying to change because others, no better informed than he, have closed their doors to him.

From what I have seen the harm to a homosexual man or woman done by the person's trying to convert is multifold. Homosexuals should be warned. First of all, the venture is almost certain to fail, and you will lose time and money. But this is the least of it. In trying to convert, you will deepen your belief that you are one of nature's misfortunes. You will intensify your clinging to conventionality, enlarge your fear and guilt and regret. You will be voting in your own mind for the premise that people should all act and feel the same ways. You will stultify your fantasy, which draws on images from your present outlook; and by the time you stop trying to change, time will be lost, and it may take you years to believe in individuality once more. Your attempt to convert is an assault on your right to do what you want so long as it harms no one, your right to give and receive love, or sensual pleasure without love, in the manner you wish to.

It ought to be considered too that there are no specialists able to restore opportunities to an aged person who has forgone his chances for erotic experience, together with its enrichments, and is now dying. In the event of this, the specialists have nothing to offer, because their leverage is in talking about the future, in making dire predictions about how people are going to be harmed by their homosexuality, and how society is going to be weakened. The truth, that the experts were only guessing, can sometimes emerge too late—and along with it, the horrendous implication that too much was staked on the conjectures of other people.

For those troubled by the existence of homosexuals, the solution must be to desist from sadistic acts and to examine the sources of their distress. To remedy this distress has both psychological value for the person and ethical importance for mankind. The "homosexual problem" as I have described it here, is the problem of condemning variety in human existence. If one cannot enjoy the fact of this variety, at the very least one must learn to accept its existence, since obviously it is here to stay.

REFERENCES

ALLPORT, GORDON, *The Nature of Prejudice*. Reading, Addison-Wesley, 1954.

BANDURA, ALBERT, *Principles of Behavior Modification*. New York, Holt, Rinehart & Winston, 1969.

BARKER, J. C., "Behavior Therapy for Transvestism: A Comparison of Pharmacological and Electrical Aversion Techniques." *Brit. J. Psychiat.*, 3 (1965), 268-276.

BARKER, J. C., THORPE, J. G., BLAKEMORE, C. B., LAVIN, N. J., and CONWAY, C. G., "Behavior Therapy in a Case of Transvestism." *Lancet*, 1 (1961), 510.

BIEBER, IRVING, *A Psychoanalytic Study of Male Homosexuality*. New York, Basic Books, 1962.

BRADY, J. P., "Brevital Relaxation Treatment of Frigidity." *Behav. Res. Ther.*, 4 (1966), 71.

CHURCHILL, WAINWRIGHT, *Homosexual Behavior Among Males*. New York, Hawthorn Books, 1967.

CLARK, D. F., "Fetishism Treated by Negative Conditioning." *Brit. J. Psychiat.*, 1963, 404-7.

COOPER, A. J., "A Case of Fetishism and Impotence Treated by Behavior Therapy." *Brit. J. Psychiat.*, 109 (1963), 649-652.

CORY, DONALD WEBSTER, *The Homosexual in America*. New York, Greenberg, 1951.

CORY, DONALD WEBSTER, ed., *Homosexuality: A Cross Cultural Approach.* New York, Julian Press, 1956.

EYSENCK, H. J., ed., *Experiments in Behavior Therapy.* New York, Pergamon Press, 1964.

FELDMAN, M. P., and MAC CULLOCH, M. J., "A Systematic Approach to the Treatment of Homosexuality by Conditioned Aversion: Preliminary Report." *Amer. J. Psychiat.,* 121 (1964), 167-172.

—— "The Application of Anticipatory Avoidance Learning to the Treatment of Homosexuality." *Behavior Res. and Therapy,* (1965), 165-183.

FLUCKIGER, FRITZ, "Through a Glass Darkly: An Evaluation of the Bieber Study on Homosexuality." *The Ladder, 10* (1966), numbers 10, 11, 12.

FREUD, SIGMUND, *Collected Papers,* ed. James Strachey, London, The Hogarth Press, 1956.

—— "Letter to an American Mother." *Amer. J. Psychiat.,* 107 (1951), 786-7.

FREUND, K., "Problems in the Treatment of Homosexuality." In H. J. Eysenck, ed., *Behavior Therapy and the Neurosis.* Oxford, Pergamon Press, 1960.

GLOVER, E., "Critical Notive of Wolpe's 'Psychotherapy by Reciprocal Inhibition.'" *Brit. J. Psychol.,* 32 (1959), 68-74.

GOLD, S., and NEUFELD, I. L., "A Learning Approach to the Treatment of Homosexuality." *Behav. Res. Ther.,* 2 (1965), 201-204.

GUARDO, CAROL, "Personal Space in Children." *Child Development, 40* (1969), 143-151.

HATTERER, LAWRENCE, *Changing Homosexuality in the Male.* New York, McGraw-Hill, 1970.

HESS, E. H., SELTZER, A. L., and SHLIEN, J. M., "Pupil Response of Hetero- and Homosexual Males to Pictures of Men and Women. A Pilot Study." *Journal of Social and Abnormal Psych.,* 70 (1965), 165-8.

HOFFMAN, MARTIN, *The Gay World.* New York, Basic Books, 1968.

HOOKER, EVELYN, "Male Homosexuals and Their Worlds." In J. Marmor, ed., *Sexual Inversion.* New York, Basic Books, 1965.

JAMES, B., "Case of Homosexuality Treated by Aversion Therapy." *Brit. Med. J.,* 1 (1962), 768.

KAMENY, FRANKLIN, From dialogue during subcommittee meeting, "Amending District of Columbia Charitable Solicitations Act." August 8, 1963.

—— "Gay is Good." In Ralph Weltge, ed., *The Same Sex.* United Church Press, 1969.

KRAFT, T., "A Case of Homosexuality Treated by Systematic Desensitization." *Amer. J. Psychother., 21* (1967), 815-821.

LURIE, E., "The Endocrine Factors in Homosexuality." *Amer. J. Science, 208* (1944), 176.

MC CONAGHY, N., "Penile Volume Change to Moving Pictures of Male and Female Nudes in Heterosexual and Homosexual Males." *Behavior Research and Therapy, 5* (1967), 43-48.

MC GUIRE, R. J., and VALLANCE, M., "Aversion Therapy by Electric Shock: A Simple Technique." *Brit. Med. J., 1* (1964), 151.

MILLER, ISABEL, *A Place for Us.* New York, McGraw-Hill, 1972.

MILLETT, KATE, *Sexual Politics.* New York, Doubleday and Company, 1970.

NICHOLS, JACK, and CLARKE, LIGE, *I Have More Fun With You Than Anybody.* New York, St. Martin's Press, 1972.

RACKMAN, S., "Sexual Disorders and Behavior Therapy." *Amer. J. of Psychiat., 118* (1961), 235-240.

RAYMOND, M. J., "Case of Fetishism Treated by Aversion Therapy." *British Medical Journal, 2* (1956), 254-257.

ROEDER, FRITZ D., "Homosexuality Burned Out." *Medical World News,* Sep 23, 1970.

RUBENSTEIN, L. H., from a paper presented at the Symposium on Homosexuality held jointly by the Medical and Social Psychology sections of the British Psychological Society, 1956.

RUBIN, ISADORE, *Homosexuals Today.* New York, Health Publications, 1965.

RUITENBEEK, HENDRICK, ed., *The Problem of Homosexuality in Modern Society.* New York, E. P. Dutton and Co., 1963.

SCHOFFIELD, *Sociological Aspects of Homosexuality.* Boston, Little, Brown and Company, 1965.

SOLYOM, L., and MILLER, S., "A Differential Conditioning Procedure as the Initial Phase of the Behavior Therapy of Homosexuality." *Behavior Res. Ther., 3* (1965).

STEVENSON and WOLPE, "Recovery from Sexual Deviations Through Overcoming Non-Sexual Neurotic Responses." *Am. J. Psychiat., 116* (1960), 737-742.

SZASZ, THOMAS, "Legal and Moral Aspects of Homosexuality." In J. Marmor, ed., *Sexual Inversion*. New York, Basic Books, 1965.

—— *Law, Liberty and Psychiatry*. New York, Collier Books, 1968.

—— *The Manufacture of Madness*. New York, Harper and Row, 1970.

TAYLOR, G. RATTRAY, *Sex in History*. New York, Vanguard, 1960.

THORPE, J. G., SCHMIDT, E., and CASTELL, D., "A Comparison of Positive and Negative (Aversive) Conditioning in the Treatment of Homosexuality." *Behav. Res. Ther., 1* (1963), 357.

TRIPP

TOBIN, KAY, *The Gay Crusaders*. New York, Paperback Library, 1971.

ULLMAN, L. P., and KRASNER, L., *Case Studies in Behavior Modification*. New York, Holt, Rinehart & Winston, 1965.

WEINBERG, GEORGE, *The Action Approach: How Your Personality Developed and How You Can Change It*. New York, Signet, 1970.

WOLPE, JOSEPH, *Psychotherapy by Reciprocal Inhibition*. Stanford, Stanford University Press, 1958.

WYDEN, PETER, and WYDEN, BARBARA, *Growing up Straight*. New York, Signet, 1968.

YATES, AUBREY, *Behavior Therapy*. New York, John Wiley & Sons, 1970.

NEWSPAPERS MENTIONED

The Advocate. Published biweekly by Advocate Publications, Inc., Box 74695, Los Angeles, California, 90004.

Gay. Published biweekly by Four Swords, Inc., P.O. Box 431, Old Chelsea Station, New York, New York 10011.

INDEX